THE PEOPLE MANAGER
A Guide for First-Time Managers

Joanna Root
Dean Hume

Copyright © 2020 Joanna Root & Dean Hume

All rights reserved

Editor: Jennifer Stout

Proof-readers: Yuliya Dray, Will Shepherd, Paolo Rigiroli

Headshot Photography: Ashton Mason

February 2020: First Edition

The cover image and related trade dress are copyright of Joanna Root and Dean Hume.

All illustrations in this book are copyright of Joanna Root.

Fonts used Lil Stuart & Hatsch Sans by Alphabeta.

While every precaution has been taken in the preparation of this book, the authors assumes no responsibility for errors or omissions, or for damages resulting from the use of information contained herein.

Jo:
For Joshua & Isabella.

Dean:
For Pippa.

Be confident. Be curious. Be kind.

About the Authors

Joanna Root is a Senior Program Manager at EA with over 20 years' experience managing people and leading and growing Agile teams. Her career path has taken her through many areas of the computer games industry, through Marketing, Developer Relations, People and Project Management. She champions Agile best practises and is passionate about coaching and supporting the teams she works with.

Dean Hume is a Senior Engineering Manager at EA with a background in building high performing teams in many different industries and sectors. He is the author of *Building Great Startup Teams* and *Progressive Web Apps* and is passionate about growing leaders and helping teams.

Preface

This book has been a long time in the making. Not just because of the physical time it took to put the chapters together, but the years we've spent actually doing the role of People Manager ourselves, experiencing the highs and the lows (including making mistakes!) and learning lessons along the way. All of which have shaped this book.

When we first started our roles as People Managers, we wished that we had a helpful resource to guide us through our early days. We truly hope this book will be a companion that provides you with the guidelines and equip you with the tools to use along your journey as a People Manager.

We want to take this opportunity to thank all the people we have collaborated with during our careers, especially the teams we have worked with as People Managers. Working alongside you has helped us grow, refine and improve our skills as managers. Without you, we would not be where we are today...the authors of this very book!

We hope you enjoy reading this as much as we did writing it!

Jo   Dean

Foreword

It is both an honour and a privilege to manage people within an organisation. The role of People Manager is a critical one and serves as the lynchpin to the worker experience. When done well, an effective People Manager truly helps a person bring their best to their role and their organisation. Joanna and Dean understand this deeply, and this philosophy has served as the foundation for their book.

The authors approach the subject of being a first-time People Manager with empathy and wisdom. Many people step into this role because of organisational need and very often feel unprepared for what's ahead. This book provides a strong framework for the role and lays out in clear and effective terms both the journey of becoming an effective manager along with deep insights on the most salient topics. It starts by asking the reader to reflect on who they are as a person, what's required of the role and how to bring these two elements together. The best managers are confident in who they are and operate from their values.

The reader is provided with a strong suite of tools, skills and tips they can use to achieve success as a manager of others. The writing is warm and friendly, and the advice is practical with relatable stories and anecdotes. There is particularly good support for some of the toughest moments of being a manager, such as delivering hard feedback, resolving conflict in your team, managing underperformance or making the difficult decision to move someone off the team.

Each chapter ends with a concise summary of takeaways as well as other sources of high-quality information so that readers can dig deeper into the topic at hand. Ultimately, this is not just a must-read for new managers but an ongoing reference throughout the manager journey.

Mala Singh
Chief People Officer
Electronic Arts

Contents

1 THE PEOPLE MANAGER — 18

- Who this book is for — 20
- How to read this book — 20
- Understanding your values — 22
- What separates a great leader from an average one? — 25
  - Empathy — 25
  - Leadership — 26
  - A manager or a friend? — 27
  - Management styles — 29
- Summary — 33

2 YOUR NEW ROLE — 36

- You're a manager...now what?! — 38
- Understanding the change in your day-to-day work life — 39
  - Superheroes need not apply! — 40
- "New role vs old role" dilemmas — 42
  - What does being a manager mean for you (and your team)?
  - Aligning with your team
  - Looking out for your team
- Establishing a 90-day plan — 48
- Looking beyond 90 days — 48
- Summary — 50
  - 51

3 GETTING TO KNOW YOUR TEAM — 55

- The People Manager loop — 58
    - Daily
    - Weekly
    - Yearly
    - The loop
- Managing teams — 59
- First-day jitters — 60
    - Getting to know each other
    - The power of one-to-ones
    - Eat with the team!
    - The "wait and see" approach
- Inheriting an established team — 66
- A remote team — 68
    - Encourage sharing
    - Keep in mind what it feels like to be remote
- The importance of the one-to-one — 71
    - Why bother with yet another meeting?
    - Tips for setting up successful one-to-ones
- What comes next? — 77
- Summary — 78

4 PERFORMANCE MANAGEMENT — 80

- The power of praise — 82
    - How and when to give praise
    - Celebrating the small things
    - Praise and personal growth
- The process of giving feedback — 89
    - Feedback "no no's" — 90

- o The BEER model of giving feedback — 91
- Creating performance plans — 92
  - o What kind of goals should be included?
  - o How do you measure progress toward goals?
- How to continuously develop your reports
  - o 70:20:10: a model for continuous learning — 96
- Summary — 100

5 ROUGH SEAS AHEAD — 102

- Dealing with conflict — 105
  - o Conflict amongst team members
  - o Conflict with a direct report
- Difficult conversations — 112
- Coaching or leading through tough situations — 113
- Performance improvement plans — 116
- Being liked as a manager — 118
  - o What if your reports used to be your teammates?
- If at first you don't succeed? — 120
- Trying a different approach — 121
- Summary — 124

6 GROWING YOUR TEAM — 126

- Why hiring matters — 128
  - o Create a plan
  - o Develop a good relationship with your recruiter
  - o Respond quickly
  - o Get the team involved

- Finding the right person — 131
- Your new hire — 133
    - Build a rock-solid onboarding process
    - Procure the correct equipment before day one
    - Build a list of FAQs
    - Assign a buddy
    - Grab lunch or a coffee
    - Create a new employee questionnaire
- Core values — 139
- What does this mean for me? — 141
- Summary — 142

7 IMPROVING YOURSELF — 144

- Feedback — 146
- The importance of continuous improvement — 147
- Coaching and mentoring — 151
    - The difference between coaching and mentoring
    - Is this really for me?
    - Becoming a mentee
    - Working with a coach
- Learning and growing — 157
    - Books
    - Conferences
    - Online learning
- Maintaining perspective
- Summary — 159

8 MAINTAINING A HIGH-PERFORMING TEAM   164

- The People Manager loop   166
- Talent reviews   167
    - The 9-box grid
- 360 Feedback   170
    - Delivering 360 Feedback to an employee
- The power of praise   174
- Motivating others   175
- Summary   177

9 LOOKING TO THE FUTURE   178

- Key takeaways   180
    - 1 to 1s/1:1s/one-to-ones
    - The power of praise
    - Don't lose your cool
    - Be yourself
    - Great People Managers care about hiring
    - Staying positive
    - Never stop learning!
- Summary   189

Chapter 1

THE PEOPLE MANAGER

Congratulations, you've just become a People Manager! This important and hugely satisfying role covers a wide range of skills and competencies, from coaching, training, communicating and leading to handling diplomacy, change, conflict and (of course) people! If you're ready to learn more about how to become a great People Manager, you're in the right place. We look forward to sharing our own experiences, ideas, good practises and practical methods to help you on your new journey.

In this chapter, we'll start by defining what your personal values are and how they fit into the context of being a People Manager. We'll also dive into what separates a great leader from an average one and finish up with the importance of management styles and how to define yours.

Who this book is for

This book has been written for those who are new to People Management or who have taken on new line reporting responsibilities. However, it is by no means limited to those who have no previous experience in this job functionality. Perhaps you've joined a new company with a different kind of team to what you've managed in the past and want to refresh your thinking about what "good" People Management looks like. Or maybe you took a career break and want to learn more about how your role can be enriched with different work practises. Whatever your level of interest or knowledge, we hope to give you a new set of practical tools and ideas to help you learn, grow and succeed in your role as a People Manager.

How to read this book

Individual chapters will help you through each stage of your growth as a People Manager, the idea being that you can refer back to different sections depending on your current stage. This book isn't intended to be read front to back like a novel; rather, you can open any chapter and read it in a modular fashion. We hope it becomes your very best friend, a trusted ally as you take your first steps into becoming a People Manager.

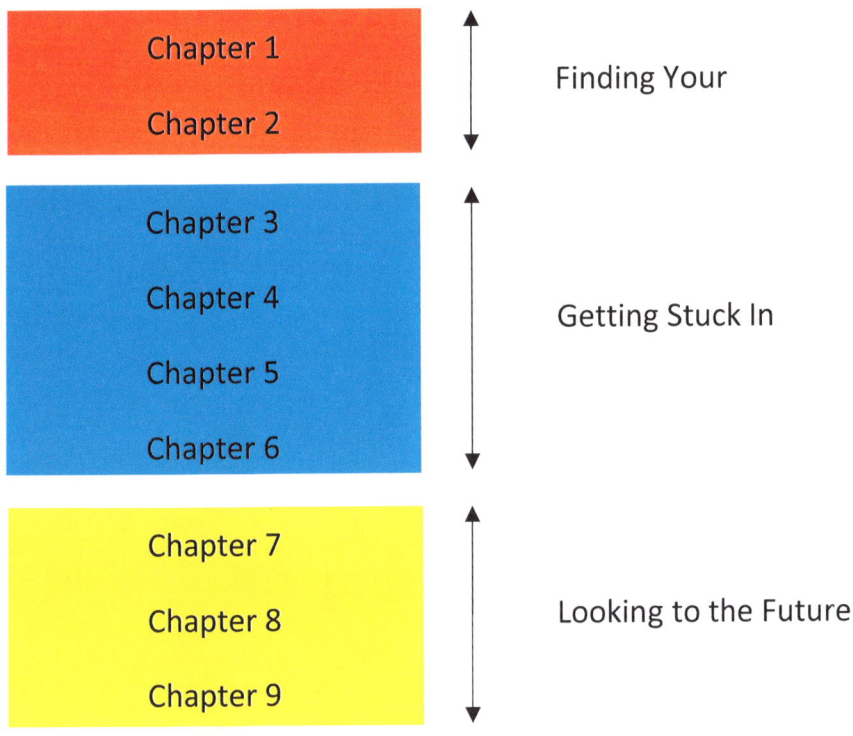

Figure 1.1 This book is broken down into three distinct parts: Finding Your Feet, Getting Stuck In and Looking to the Future.

This book is divided into three key stages, as Figure 1.1 shows. The first two chapters explore the early steps and advice you might take to **Find Your Feet**. Next, we dive into the more practical side of things and **Get Stuck In** to the practical side of managing people. Finally, we **Look to the Future** and discover how you as a People Manager can ensure that you're continually improving yourself as well as those around you. We've mapped each of the chapters in the book according to the three key stages of your growth.

Understanding your values

Before we go any further, let's pause for a second and consider how personal values fit into the context of being a People Manager. What do we mean by "values"? Our values are what we use when we evaluate big decisions; they determine how we deal with the *consequences* of those decisions.

Most of our daily decisions are based on "gut feelings", learnt behaviours and things we internalise on a subconscious level. When making these decisions, our personal values influence us even though we aren't intentionally using them.

As humans, the experiences that we've had in life, along with the way we've been brought up, educated and socialised, influence how we make decisions, even if we don't realise (or like) it! This is especially true for the People Manager. What drives you? What makes you tick? How are you motivated? How do you feel valued? What is important to you? By really understanding your own values, you can turn these "gut feelings" into something more intentional that you *do* think about before acting. You can understand why your values lead you to evaluate certain decisions and behaviours. Your values can become your north star, your guiding principles.

It might seem early in this book to start talking about homework, but before we go any further, let's take a look at Figure 1.2.

List of Values

Accountability	Freedom	Patience
Achievement	Friendship	Patriotism
Adaptability	Fun	Peace
Adventure	Future generations	Personal fulfillment
Altruism	Generosity	Power
Ambition	Giving back	Pride
Authenticity	Grace	Recognition
Balance	Gratitude	Reliability
Beauty	Growth	Resourcefulness
Being the best	Harmony	Respect
Belonging	Health	Responsibility
Career	Home	Risk taking
Caring	Honesty	Safety
Collaboration	Hope	Security
Commitment	Humility	Self-discipline
Community	Humour	Self-expression
Compassion	Inclusion	Self-respect
Competence	Independence	Serenity
Confidence	Initiative	Service
Connection	Integrity	Spirituality
Contribution	Job security	Sportsmanship
Cooperation	Joy	Success
Courage	Justice	Teamwork
Creativity	Kindness	Thrift
Curiosity	Knowledge	Time
Dignity	Leadership	Tradition
Diversity	Learning	Travel
Environment	Legacy	Trust
Efficiency	Leisure	Truth
Equality	Love	Understanding
Ethics	Loyalty	Uniqueness
Excellence	Making a difference	Usefulness
Fairness	Nature	Vision
Faith	Openness	Wealth
Family	Optimism	Well-being
Financial stability	Parenting	Wisdom

This list of values comes from the book *Dare to Lead* by Brené Brown[1]. It's meant to serve as a guide to assist your thought process, but there might be other values not listed here that you could use as well.

Set aside a few minutes to work through this list, picking three values that most appeal to you and what you think *you* value. This list is quite lengthy (we've tried doing this exercise and choosing only three is much harder than you think!), but it can help you prioritise what really matters to you. After some deliberation and short-listing, Dean chose *Belonging*, *Fun* and *Teamwork* as his top three personal values, while Jo narrowed hers down to *Recognition*, *Integrity* and *Collaboration*.

Once you have your values narrowed down to three, reflect on them and keep them in mind as you progress through the book. It's important to realise that everything in your life up until this point has sewn together what matters to you and created your core values. If you're able to articulate these values, you can practise and stand by them. We have both found that by identifying the values we feel are important to us, we are able to use them as a guide or an influence on the way we act as People Managers. We have also found that we unconsciously "live" these values in our day-to-day work, and when looking back at why we handled situations in the way that we did, we can see how our values played an influential part. At other times, we purposefully seek outcomes that hold true to our values: they provide a "guiding light", a reminder to maintain consistency and effectiveness. As you read on, you'll find out how your own values will play a big role in working effectively and closely with people. Whether you're faced with good times or tough challenges, understanding and embracing your values will be the key to setting yourself up for success. With your values in mind, you'll be well-equipped to deal with decisions knowing that you'll make choices consistent with what's ultimately important to you.

What separates a great leader from an average one?

Before you answer this question, think of your own past managers or leaders. Were they all fabulous? There's a good chance that one or two of them will stand out because they *weren't* fabulous! Can you remember how you felt about having a manager who wasn't that great? It probably affected your motivation to get up and go to work, your enthusiasm to be productive, your energy to thrive and your ability to succeed.

On the flip side, if you've had a great manager, you'll probably remember feeling confident in your role, positive and happy about coming to work and able to perform your job in a productive and effective way.

Being a great leader is important for your business, the team that you're responsible for and you yourself as a new manager. It's important to realise that being a People Manager is an honour, a privilege and a great responsibility. Whether you realise it or not, how you present yourself directly impacts the business strategy of your organisation because it plays an important part in engaging, developing and retaining talent. We also know that doing it well is hard work - there's no getting away from this!

As the saying goes, "what you reap is what you sow", and this is especially relevant in the case of the People Manager. By adopting, learning and constantly improving the skills needed to do a great job as a manager, you'll boost confidence amongst your team members and set an example of the behaviours, positivity and professionalism you want your direct reports to demonstrate.

Empathy

One skill that's sometimes overlooked by managers (or let's just say the "average" manager) is empathy. Whilst not the most obvious skill needed to be an effective manager or leader, the benefits it can bring to the role are invaluable. Empathetic managers try to see situations from the perspective of others, which prevents them from jumping to conclusions or making assumptions and decisions too quickly. If you take the time (in a time-starved environment) to listen to and understand the different opinions at play, you let your reports know that you *do* care what they think and feel, that their points of view have equal importance to you and within the team. Finding out what is important to other people also gives you more information to do your job more effectively. You can make informed decisions or choices that have substance to them. Too much information is never a problem for a manager, but too little sure can be.

Leadership

Should a "great manager" be a "great leader", too? Leadership often seems daunting to new managers, which isn't surprising. When we think about great leaders, we tend to imagine tough CEO types: people in charge of huge businesses and budgets who might be distanced from employees at the coalface.

Let's strip it back a bit and talk about what leadership actually means. Take this quote from the MAS – Management Advisory Service[2]:

"A good leader takes the lead. A good leader has personality, courage, clear vision with ambition to succeed. A good leader encourages the team to perform to their optimum all the time and drives organisational success".

This quote really gets to the core of what makes a leader: the people that this person is leading. As a manager or as a leader, you're encouraging *people*. You're coaching, listening, advising, problem-solving and facilitating, not laying down the law, giving out instructions, ignoring feedback and creating a void between yourself and the team. By always putting your team first and understanding their personalities, motivations, skills and preferences, you're encouraging them to be their best. High-performing, motivated and happy employees ultimately enable their organisations to perform well and achieve success.

Figure 1.3 I'm not bossy! I have.......leadership skills! Understand?

A manager or a friend?

If you were already on a team before becoming its manager, you might have some good friendships in place with the people who are now going to be your direct reports. If you're new to the business, making friends with your colleagues might seem like a good move: surely the confidence you're going to need to springboard into your managerial role will come from forging friendships at work? You'd be forgiven for thinking that friendship goes hand-in-hand with building a new team, but good People Managers and great leaders usually demonstrate empathy, soft skills and coaching ability without necessarily being best friends with everyone on the team!

However, think again of previous managers you've worked with, liked and respected. Did you count them as friends? Discussing career aspirations, promotion, salary and personal development with a People Manager is certainly the nuts and bolts of a structured and professional working relationship. However, to really understand your team members, a deeper level of discussion will naturally have to take place. And once you start talking about role preferences, personal attributes, learning opportunities, feedback and project nuances, you may feel that the boundary between manager and friend becomes less defined.

No one is suggesting that the only way to coach a direct report well is to become that person's friend. Great managers earn team trust over time. Empathy shows your team members that you "get" them, that you understand their workplace achievements and disappointments. Listening (or even just being available to listen) is often all that is needed when people hit difficult periods in their careers. As a People Manager, you can and should look for opportunities to coach and encourage, acknowledge and praise, boost and motivate. But another part of your role is to act as a counterweight: you might have to share negative feedback (more on that in Chapter 5), initiate a performance management discussion or encounter difficult or serious personnel scenarios. This is where you'll be glad for the boundary you established between being a manager and becoming a friend.

You may also find yourself involved with or party to confidential or sensitive conversations. Being a confidant for your team members can be a positive and rewarding part of being a manager, but not every manager will feel comfortable with this responsibility. Be mindful that although you might want to be the point of contact for your reports when they experience difficult situations in their professional or personal lives, you're not expected to handle everything that's thrown at you. Your business is likely to have Human Resources (HR) representatives who can guide or advise you, or step in when you feel like you're out of your depth.

It's important that you ask for help if you need it; HR policies, processes and support exist for this very reason. Being a manager doesn't mean being a superhero (or at least not all the time, although we do like the costumes)!

Management styles

It's relatively easy to choose one particular leadership style and assume (or hope) that it works for everybody. But remember, as a *People* Manager, your role is all about individuals, which means a wide range of personalities, traits, habits and motivators. It's rare for one style to suit everyone. Thinking about your previous managers will give you a good starting point for the management (or coaching) style you want to bring to your new role. It's okay to dial your style up or down, nothing is set in stone here! In fact, flexibility is one of the unsung heroes of People Management.

Feedback and continuous improvement are the keys to good teamwork, and there's no reason why they can't help you fine-tune your management style. As part of getting to know your new team, consider asking them what a good manager looks like from their perspective. If they can help you formulate a style that works, you stand a much better chance of creating a healthy, motivated and happy group of direct reports.

Here are some questions to get you started:

How can I help you work well/better?

This may seem too open-ended, but it can flag up some easy wins for you as a new manager. For example, anything from "my PC is too slow" or "my colleague's music is too loud" to "I need more money" or "I never talk to my manager" will give you tremendous insight into both team member motivation and how to improve it.

How important do you feel it is to be acknowledged (and/or rewarded) for good work?

We aren't necessarily talking about bonus time, although everyone likes a bonus! This question will help you learn what motivates your reports and how they respond to praise or acknowledgement. The form of praise or reward is also important: positive 360 Feedback from peers and colleagues, public thanks from senior management or a team dinner are just some of the ways we've been able to acknowledge good work because we took the time to understand how people feel appreciated.

What do or don't you like in a manager?

This gets straight to the point, and team members who have had good or bad experiences in the past will be able to give you answers straight away. Just as how we suggested that you recall good or bad managers in your past, this question helps you learn what styles work for your team. "Micromanagement" may be a complaint; "controlling" or "bossy" might be another. Dig and ask why! Try to learn how these negative behaviours were demonstrated and what their impact was. For example, being "left alone" might be cited as a good trait, but only because it's the perceived solution to being micromanaged. If "having regular one-to-ones" is something that your team members like, drill down further to find out what "regular" means and what they want to discuss during these sessions.

You might not agree with or want to adopt all the feedback and suggestions that you hear, but asking your team for their input lets them know that you value their opinion and helps you make a confident start. Who *wouldn't* want to know the behaviours and styles that will best suit the people they're responsible for?

> *You don't know what you don't know unless you ask.*

Whatever your management style and however diverse your team might be, being able to maintain a professional, unbiased or impartial relationship with your direct reports is crucial for your success. Being a respected, open, honest and fair leader whilst maintaining team respect and trust is the sign of a great manager!

Figure 1.4 Which management style do you think is more effective?!

We hope that we've whet your appetite for learning more about your new role. There's plenty to do and lots to learn, but we're here to help! The next chapter awaits…are you coming with us?

Summary

- This book is intended to help anyone who's new (or returning) to the role of People Manager. It's a collection of advice, coaching tips and real-life experiences and anecdotes. You aren't alone, we're here to help you succeed!
- Introduce yourself! If people don't know you, how can you expect to find out more about them?
- Get to know your team - individually or as a whole - by using an approach that suits you both, from team discussion to one-to-one chats to on-the-job observation.
- Learn how your team works. Is it project-based or people-centric? Positive and productive or negative and checked-out?
- Think about what makes a great leader and the skills or attributes you might engage to get to "great" instead of "average".
- Being a "great mate" to the people on your team isn't always the best approach for a new manager. Work out what kind of a People Manager you want to be by using past examples from your own career. Think about the challenges you might face as a People Manager and consider how you could handle them if your style was more friendly than professional.
- Don't be afraid to ask for suggestions and input about what makes a good or bad manager. Your team members want you to succeed, so ask them to tell you what matters to *them*.

References

1. *Dare to Lead* by Brené Brown - Penguin Books - 2018
2. *What Makes a Good Leader* - MAS - http://www.mas.org.uk/management-advisory-service/what-makes-a-good-leader.html

YOUR NEW ROLE

Chapter 2

One of the biggest challenges that new managers face is determining the first steps they need to take in their new role. In this chapter, we'll explore what it is that People Managers do and why it's so important to take a mental break from your previous position. We'll also look at how you can formulate a plan for the coming weeks and months ahead.

You're a manager...now what!?

When you first take on the role of People Manager, it can feel like you're being handed the keys to a castle. Free reign is *yours*! Well, not exactly: there's a lot of responsibility that comes with being a People Manager but often very little detail as to what is actually expected of you. You might be handed a job specification or maybe a list of the role's goals and metrics, but it's highly unlikely you'll receive instructions on how to actually jump in and do the job, or what kind of a People Manager you should be! Let's unpick the challenge of finding your feet in these early days. It's one thing to understand *what to do*, but the practical aspect of *actually doing it* are often two different things.

Before we go any further, let's highlight some of the steps that a new

People Manager might take that we'll be exploring in this chapter:

- Accept that things will change in your day-to-day work life
- Recognise the change of focus from your old role and your new one going forward
- Align with your team and champion their best interests
- Build a 90-day plan to help you kickstart this new phase of your career

Understanding the change in your day-to-day work life

A lot of this chapter applies to what you would do if you started at a company in a brand-new role, but let's take a look at what happens when you're promoted within your existing company to this brand-new role. If you've already stepped into a new position, you might have noticed that things are a little different to how they were in your previous role. People now look to you for answers, you're responsible for your team…not to mention the fact that you set the example going forward. This can seem like a scary proposition! Perhaps you were an integrated part of a project team or helped build "things" in your last role; it can be tough to stop doing what you've been doing for the past several years and suddenly do something quite different.

When I switched from software engineer to manager, I really missed the challenge of building and creating things. I was a "maker". At first, it felt like I wasn't contributing anything useful anymore, but eventually I came to the realisation that my job was now the team and their success. I needed to stop thinking about what I was missing out on and concentrate on ensuring that the team had everything they needed to be productive and successful.

Another transitional challenge I faced was how to handle my team members: many of my new reports were previously my peers, and now, all of a sudden, I was responsible for their careers. To say this was scary would be an understatement! It was important for me to take a mental break from my old job in order to give the people I was responsible for the best chance to do what I expected of them.

Superheroes need not apply!

Apart from still trying to do their old job, many first-time managers still feel a bit awkward when it comes to delegating or managing their former peers. If you let this dominate your management style, you'll quickly find yourself either overloaded or micromanaging your team. You'll not only stress out your employees, but yourself, too!

If you've been working with your peers for a while, you probably know them pretty well by this point, which means you know their strengths and weaknesses. You're also in the best position to delegate activities from your previous role to help your team both grow and gain autonomy to learn new things.

From personal experience, we know that it can be really hard to let go of work, especially if it's not done the way that you would do it. It might mean that it takes longer or that mistakes get made at first, but that's okay: this is all part of your team's learning process. Step back and trust others to complete the work in their way. You'll find that once the ball is rolling, things will start to get faster and faster as your people grow and learn. Continuous feedback is a great tool to help with this (we'll talk more about that in Chapter 4).

In his book *High Output Management*, Andy Groves (former chairman and CEO of Intel) talks about his approach to delegation[1]:

> *"A given managerial approach is not equally effective under all conditions".*

With this quote in mind, it's worth remembering that the way you delegate isn't a one-size-fits-all dictation: everyone's different. It's important to step back and trust your team to complete the work, but it's also important that you keep a pulse-check on projects and use regular check-ins to see how your team members are doing. In Chapter 3, we'll take a closer look at one-to-one meetings and how you can tailor them to take delegated tasks into account.

"New role vs old role" dilemmas

It can be hard to realign your expectations if your previous role was more hands-on and you produced high-quality work on a regular basis. Many first-time leaders feel a sense of guilt when they realise that they aren't contributing as much as they used to. Don't worry, this is completely natural! Your day-to-day job function has changed, but the skills you've honed up until now will still be as valuable to your development as they were before, you're just going to add more strings to your bow and learn different things. Previously, you were probably thinking introspectively - how you could be the best version of yourself for the business or role you were in. Now, you're going to be thinking about your team as well as yourself - extending your sphere of influence to help others be their best, while at the same time learning and growing in your own skin.

Contrary to what you might think, your team don't expect you to keep on doing your old job and the new one at the same time. After all, you're not a circus juggler! It's worth remembering that, as a manager, you can't focus on individual tasks - you have to realign your efforts to help your team complete their assignments. It's a subtle shift in mindset, but it's important to remember that your success is inextricably tied to your ability to help your team succeed.

This is probably sounding both confusing and daunting at this point: what is this new all-singing, all-dancing role you've decided to take on? How is it even possible to focus on a team while you're adapting your own skills and learning how to refocus on the new job at hand? As we've just talked about, the first step is simply to accept that things will change in your day-to-day work life. You'll need to make time to understand what's required, not only from your new role but from your reports and the wider business, too. Jumping straight in and making sweeping changes might feel like the best thing to do initially, but it could come back to bite you later. Imagine moving into a new house and immediately knocking down some walls and adding new windows and doors before you've even sorted out where to put the furniture! Wouldn't it make more sense to get a sense of what works and what doesn't, draw up a list of requirements and start with the most important? Yes, it's a simplistic comparison, but becoming a new People Manager gives you a blank canvas to start afresh, to pull what you know and what you don't know together with what you need to learn and change and how you're going to get there.

What does being a manager mean for you (and your team)?

If you think that leading is about power, then being a People Manager might not be the best role for you! While it's important to take a mental break from your old role, it's also important to remember that in most organisations the people you manage work *with you*, not *for you*. Becoming a People Manager doesn't suddenly mean that you're better or superior to your previous role: it simply means that your team now look to you for direction. Some of the most brilliant leaders we've worked with have been kind, generous, open and honest. You'll quickly find that by treating your team in the same way you'd like to be treated, they'll enjoy coming to work (and having you as their manager). Happier team members are much more productive!

Aligning with your team

So how do you get there? At a practical level - and depending on how your day is spent - this might mean you find yourself in a lot more meetings. No one likes a day filled with them, but sometimes participating in, facilitating and leading meetings with your team will give you the best opportunity to get up to speed with how your business, your team members and your role fit together. Figure 2.1 shows what a typical day in your calendar might look like.

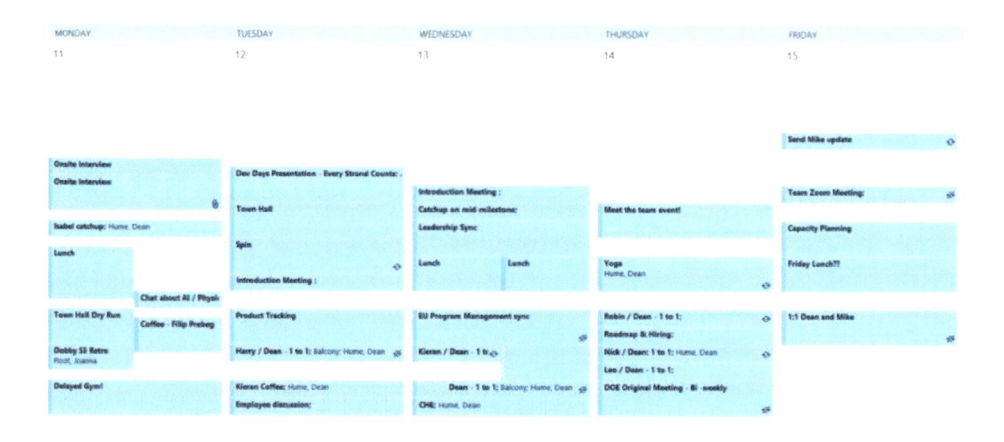

Figure 2.1 This is what the average day for a manager can look like. That's a lot of meetings!

With your days looking like this, it's easy to understand why you won't be able to contribute as much as you did before. Your new role means that you're more of a guide, supervisor and all-around "impediment remover", not to mention facilitator and enabler. Yes, these are a lot of hats to wear! Whenever we compare a new manager's role to a previously held one, we like to use the analogy of a football coach. Sure, the coach might have played football previously (and was probably quite good at it to make the team), but their job at this stage isn't to play, it's to do everything in their power through their skills and experience to help their team win games. This is now your job as a People Manager: coaching, encouraging, supporting and "winning". It also means that when the team fail, you fail, too.

If you're looking for a way to instantly gauge how you're doing, take a look at your team's health. If they're happy and succeeding, you're doing a great job! If motivation is low and tasks are being handled in a lacklustre fashion, you need to shake things up. We'll get into more detail about giving, seeking and receiving feedback in Chapter 4.

Looking out for your team

One thing that some of the best leaders we've worked with have in common is their ability to shield their teams from outside pressures and stand up for them. In any organisation, it's easy to get caught up in politics, meetings and events that aren't relevant to our daily work, and it happens across the board. This is where an effective People Manager comes in: People Managers play a critical role in supporting their teams, removing bottlenecks and getting out of the way so that team members can simply "get on with it".

So what does all of this actually *mean* on a practical level? It means that, as a manager, it's up to you to look out for your team and to support them. Closely aligning yourself with your team in order to be able to champion their best interests is one of the first steps toward building trust as their new People Manager. If you drop your team at a moment's notice or show indifference to their issues or difficulties, their motivation will start to spiral.

Close alignment with your team will also stand you in good stead if a time arises where you have to pass down information or a decision from the management team above you. This can seem especially daunting if you think it'll have a negative impact on your team (as illustrated below!)

Passing along information that you don't necessarily agree with could potentially make your reports feel like being a bird on one of the lower branches in the image above. It should be your aim to ensure that your team aren't covered in poop! The trust you build with your team can serve to shield them from external pressures. By always trying to communicate openly and clearly, explaining and discussing potentially disruptive news or messages, you can demonstrate that you have your team's best interest at heart. A close alignment can be achieved over time by showing empathy, acknowledging difficult times and always demonstrating a strong, supportive leadership ethic.

Nelson Mandela once said,

> *"It is better to lead from behind and to put others in front, especially when you celebrate victory when nice things occur. You take the front line when there is danger. Then people will appreciate your leadership".*

This couldn't be truer for a People Manager. New decisions or information can present your team with a sense of fear of the unknown, of the consequences of failure or of looking dumb. This is where the People Manager role is truly different and requires you to step up. Instead of shirking away from responsibility and leading from a distance, choose to be present; your team will take notice.

If people don't feel confident in the path ahead, it's vital that you lead by example, even if this means you disagree with a delegated decision. If your team sees you fearlessly taking on a new change, it's easier for them to be confident in following your lead. Otherwise, it can look like you're delegating to protect yourself and setting someone else up to take the fall.

When you step up and show your people a plan that you're helping to deliver, they're much more likely to buy in and believe in you.

Another important part of this equation is not expecting your team to do anything that you wouldn't do yourself. Far too often, leaders will ask things of their employees that they wouldn't dream of doing if they were in their shoes. Perhaps a tricky conversation needs to happen or a boring task needs to be undertaken. You're a manager now, so you can delegate this to someone else, it's not your problem anymore, right? Wrong! As a leader, you need to lead by example and set the example. If you *do* need to delegate, accompany that delegation with an explanation of why you're asking someone else to do it instead. People have certain expectations of leaders, and it's important that you live up to them.

Remember that in today's business world, the competition for great talent is fierce. If you don't treat your team the same way you'd like to be treated, they'll simply move on until they find a workplace that can.

Does this mean that you have to be serious and sensible all the time? Can you still have fun with your team? Of course, you can! Becoming a People Manager doesn't mean that you have to change your personality or walk on eggshells. Just be authentic. Put your best foot forward and promote yourself in the role through the skills and abilities you bring to it, rather than acting like some kind of an egotist who deserves it.

Establishing a 90-day plan

Okay, so you've got your head around (and are looking forward) to the changes that are inevitably happening. You've switched focus to the requirements of your new role, and you've also begun the important process of building a cohesive and closely aligned team. What happens next? It's time to use these new tools and draw up a plan for your first 90 days in your new role.

You might be thinking, "Why 90 days? I want to make a difference and achieve big wins sooner!" But even with the best intentions and endless enthusiasm, being a new manager can be as daunting as it is exciting. It would be unreasonable to assume that you would understand everything that's expected of you, become familiar with your new team and also meet well-defined objectives in a shorter period of time. Most companies work within or toward quarterly timescales, goals or project objectives. A three-month period to create a management structure that works both for you and your reports is a more realistic timeframe for you to see results.

A 90-day plan can look as simple or as detailed as you want, but its main purpose is to give your new role some definition and to set early goals for you to work toward. Here are some examples of actions you might want to consider including in your plan:

- Book 30-minute one-to-one meetings with every new report, either weekly or biweekly
- Organise a social event with the whole team (drinks after work, a team lunch, etc.)
- Talk with your own manager to discuss their expectations of your role and any insights they can share about people or team dynamics
- Put together a profile of your new team members that includes information you learn from one-to-one meetings, HR systems or your own observations and discussions with the wider team, e.g., career aspirations, personal motivations, skills, teamwork preferences, etc.
- Schedule regular reviews of your progress

Instead of only focusing on the immediate days and weeks ahead, try looking even further down the road. While this might include looking at the team, you might also want to look at yourself. What areas are you weak in and need to improve? Perhaps you've never run a one-to-one meeting before and need to read up about the best approach: that's the type of thing you can start jotting down in the first week in your new role. By the time you approach 30, 60 or even 90 days, you might have achieved many of your goals; some might not even make sense at that point.

Looking beyond 90 days

Imagine your business or organisational structure as a military battalion: an entry-level private might still be learning the ropes, but the next few levels of experience might be the sergeants who oversee troops of soldiers and need more operational details about the battle plan. Ascending through the ranks, each new role requires a different, more complex level of understanding of the overall mission. More responsibility and decision-making. More strategy and logistics. More critical information and dependencies. Many generals like to lead in the battlefield, but you won't find them directly on the frontline: this is because their strength lies in leading their troops to victory, which requires a strategic understanding of how the entire mission can be accomplished.

Whilst we wouldn't advocate likening your workplace to a battlefield, this analogy of organisational structure is useful for understanding the key things you need to know to succeed in your new role. Prior to becoming a manager, you may have been a "maker" who focused on daily tasks at a microlevel. In your new role, you'll need to not only look at the next few weeks ahead but start aiming high and thinking about your team over the next 3, 6 or even 12 months.

How can you continually improve both the team and yourself?

At this point, you don't need to have a crystal-clear idea of how to do this type of forward thinking, but it's smart to keep it in the back of your mind. As we move through the next chapters, you'll start to see a clearer picture of what you need to build a plan. It's worth mentioning that, as a new manager, you're already on the right track: reading books like this is the first step toward becoming a *great* People Manager.

Summary

- Your role as a People Manager is now the team and their success. Your goal is to ensure that they have everything they need to be successful.
- Make a clean mental break from your old job and prepare to take on the new one.
- As a new manager, your role involves looking out for your team and leading by example. It's also important that you don't do everything yourself and remember that the success of the team means success for you.
- Establish a plan for your first 90 days by assessing your strengths and weaknesses.
- What are your plans for the next 3, 6 or even 12 months? Formulate a bigger plan by looking ahead and ensuring that you're able to help your team grow.

References

1. *High Output Management* by Andy Grove - Vintage Books - 1995
2. *How to Lead from Behind* - Virgin - https://www.virgin.com/entrepreneur/how-lead-behind

Chapter 3

GETTING TO KNOW YOUR TEAM

Where do I start? It's the most obvious question, one that every new People Manager asks themselves (even if they don't say it out loud). You're in a new role, with a large or small team of people who have a range of expectations of you as their manager.

These expectations will be wide-ranging and diverse, including (but not limited to) personal, career, project- and team-related, performance, motivational, etc. Your new team might start to overwhelm you with questions or, conversely, take no notice of you and expect you to get straight on with the job. Take a deep breath! The most important thing for you to do at this point is to simply get to know your new team members. That's why this chapter is all about people, the most valuable part of any team. We'll explore both the different types of situations you'll face and how to build rapport. We'll also look at the importance of one-to-one meetings and why they're such an important tool.

The People Manager loop

Before we dive in, let's examine the role of a People Manager from a holistic point of view. Throughout your work life, there will be tasks and processes that you implement and follow on a daily, weekly or even yearly cadence. It's important to understand how all these pieces fit together and ideally when you should be doing what. Let's take a look at the timeline in Figure 3.1.

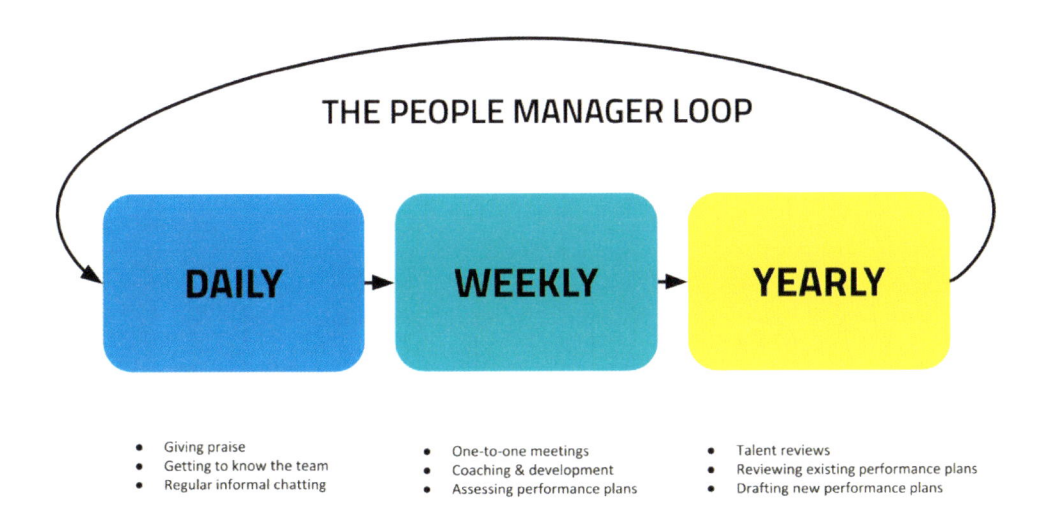

THE PEOPLE MANAGER LOOP

DAILY → **WEEKLY** → **YEARLY**

- Giving praise
- Getting to know the team
- Regular informal chatting

- One-to-one meetings
- Coaching & development
- Assessing performance plans

- Talent reviews
- Reviewing existing performance plans
- Drafting new performance plans

Figure 3.1 The People Manager loop.

This figure represents a typical schedule that you might encounter as a People Manager. Whilst different organisations might have a different cadence or order of events, in general, these are the things you can expect to be doing throughout the course of a year. Let's break them down a little and explain how we'll cover them in the chapters to come.

Daily

In your daily role, you'll learn more about your team and start to spot opportunities to praise them individually for their great work. Later in this chapter, we'll get into how to build rapport with your teams and the positive benefits that doing so can have in your daily relationships - not to mention how much it can make work feel more like fun! You'll also learn the importance of praise and the impact it can have on people (spoiler alert: praise is one of the greatest free gifts you can give).

Obvious though it may seem, busy days and lots of meetings might mean that you don't easily get the chance to chat to every member of your team. A quick hello or similar greeting at the beginning or end of the day is all it takes to keep a connection alive.

Weekly

As the days roll into weeks, there are important practical tasks in the People Manager loop that can help your team's career development and productivity. In this current chapter, we'll touch on that by describing the importance of one-to-one meetings.

Yearly

Chapter 4 cover some techniques you can use to ensure that you craft and review performance plans for each of your reports. We'll look closely at what a good plan looks like and how to measure your reports against it.

The loop

No loop would be complete without starting all over again! As you can imagine, the role of a People Manager is continuous - there's always something to do. This is why once these crucial events take place, it's important that they start all over again. The information and feedback you gain from each of these steps is taken forward when you repeat the process, to ensure that you have a wealth of insight and experience to keep on improving. Once you have a few of these under your belt, the next time gets easier and easier!

Managing teams

As you flip through the pages of this book, you might be wondering how your new role fits into the dynamic of your organisation. Perhaps you've recently joined a company and stepped into this role, or maybe you were recently promoted and need to manage a new (or old!) team. Whatever your situation, stepping into a management role amongst a group of known (or unknown) people might seem a bit scary.

The reality is that there is no handbook for dealing with people, each group brings its own thrills and challenges. As much as we both love being managers, we have to admit that people are the toughest (and most enjoyable) part of the job. No two people are the same, and the passions and personalities that make them up are just as different. There's never a right or wrong answer, either: what works for one report almost certainly doesn't work for another.

In this chapter, we'll look at some of the concepts that help us as People Managers and how you can use this knowledge to confidently approach a team (new or established, remote or local) and give them the best support under your management.

First-day jitters

Joining a new team can sometimes feel like the first morning at a new school. What will the people be like? Do they get along? Will they like me? Are they any good? All of these thoughts will probably run through your head as you approach your first day with a new team. The funny thing is that the new team probably have some of these same questions running through their own heads about you, too!

The role of a People Manager on a new team is often filled with uncertainty, and on top of that, it takes time to get to know your new team. As their manager, you need to learn about them and use your best judgement to make decisions based on what you observe. Even a *New York Times* best-selling book on people management can only give you advice, not a step-by-step guide to handling *your* team. Dealing with humans is a moving target! With that said, we'll do our best to guide you on your journey and provide our personal insights into new teams based on our own previous experience.

Getting to know each other

In your daily interactions at work, you're very likely to spend a lot of time with your team members, getting to know their professional habits, needs and experiences. Whilst the team might be successful and executing to the best of their ability, truly great leaders go a bit deeper and get a lot more back. One way to accomplish this is through the most underrated yet key part of managing people: taking the time to build rapport and trust with each person on your team.

What does "building rapport" actually mean? Put simply, it means going the extra mile to get to know the *real* person behind the team member. If you only keep your workplace interactions on a professional level, how will you ever understand what makes someone tick, what motivates them? How can you ever hope to get the best out of them? Everyone is different, but if you align their goals, the work they enjoy doing and what you need to get done, you'll be amazed at what your team can accomplish.

Now this doesn't mean that you have to be best buddies with the people who report to you, but it does mean that you need to take the time to *genuinely* find out about their background, history and interests. You may have noticed the word genuinely in that last sentence - getting to know your team shouldn't be done with personal gain in mind, this is all about growing relationships! We spend a third of our lives[1] with the people we work with. Our colleagues play such a big role in our happiness at work, it only makes sense to get to know them better.

Jo says

Believe it or not, I've actually found that when I had good rapport with the people I worked with, it was much easier to give honest feedback. This may seem counterintuitive, but people are more open to your thoughts if they trust you and feel like you "have their back".

Rapport-building with my past teams has taken place through a variety of activities. I frequently ask my reports to talk me through the work they've produced (think "show and tell"!), which gives me the opportunity to understand their achievements and offer my feedback in the moment. I'm also a big fan of having coffee with team members - conversation away from our desks helps people relax and see us as colleagues as well as managers.

Ultimately, giving your reports feedback is about helping them grow and become better at their jobs. Put yourself in their shoes: if you receive feedback from someone who knows nothing about you and you can't relate to them, it's hard to receive it sincerely!

As we've mentioned, building rapport with the people on your team is a key part of being a great People Manager, but how do you actually go about doing it? For some people, building rapport may come naturally thanks to their personality, but for others, it can take a bit of work.

Building rapport with your team is really about making that extra effort to get to know them.

Here are a few ideas to get you started:

- Ask about their hobbies and interests outside of work
- Find out about their family - do they have children? As parents, both of us are more than happy to talk about family life!
- Inquire about where they grew up
- Chat about previous jobs and what they liked (or otherwise!) about those companies and roles
- Ask them to show you something they've worked on recently that they're pleased with
- Grab coffee or lunch together and don't necessarily talk about work

It might seem like some of these are obvious and normal, but it's worth remembering the difference that talking about such simple things can make in your relationship with the team. If you aren't already doing them, give it a try; you'll notice the change in no time at all. That said, if your report doesn't seem open to this kind of conversation, it's better not to pursue it. Sometimes a manager asking what may seem like probing personal questions could have the opposite effect from what you were hoping to achieve!

The power of one-to-ones

As managers, we find that one of the best ways to inspire, engage and really understand more about the people we work with is during one-to-one meetings. Your team is a great source of information, ideas and suggestions, and team meetings are a great way to get collective feedback, but there will be times when things need to be said in private, where points of view can be expressed that might differ from everyone else's. Coaching, support and feedback need a dedicated forum that is open, honest and confidential, and this is where the one-to-one meeting proves its worth.

Try to schedule a one-to-one meeting with each of your direct reports every two weeks. This might seem like a lot of work, but it gives you an opportunity to get a feel for how the employee is doing, and it also keeps your hand on the pulse of the organisation. If you have a large number of team members reporting to you, meeting with each and every employee every two weeks might not be scalable. Work around what's achievable, but remember that these meetings should happen regularly in order for you (and your employee!) to get the best out of them. We'll take a more detailed look at the importance of one-to-ones later in the chapter.

Eat with the team!

As far-fetched as it might sound, eating together as a team can be a great way of building connections and bonds. In fact, a recent study from Cornell University found that employees who ate meals together had significantly better team performance at work than those who didn't[2]:

"Eating together is a more intimate act than looking over an Excel spreadsheet together. That intimacy spills back over into work".

If you think about it, getting together to share food, laugh and talk can only bring us closer. In fact, we often wonder if half the world's wars couldn't be solved over a good meal!

The sad truth of the modern office is that many employees will sit at their desks and continue working while eating their lunch. Encourage your team to eat together every so often, and you'll see conversation taking place and hear laughter rather than the clicking of a keyboard and zero social interaction. Many managers make the mistake of frowning upon full lunch hours - rather, you should encourage it. Of course, when the pressure's on, the team should be prepared to put in the hours, but it shouldn't be the norm for (or even an expectation of) your team to regularly skip lunch breaks. Taking a break, changing focus and diffusing the atmosphere can have an immensely positive effect on a busy or stressed team.

As a People Manager, you have the ability to influence or encourage the team in eating together. Whilst employees do need their own downtime or space away from the working environment, you might just find that a group lunch is the perfect way to build rapport with your new team and break the ice at the same time! Often, getting together outside the confines of your office space allows people to feel more relaxed and open. Plus, it gives you the opportunity to get to know the *real* people on your team, too. As their manager, you might, of course, offer to pay for the meal, but using that as a reason for getting everyone together might not be entirely genuine (you don't want to make it feel like they're obligated or forced to meet with you on their downtime).

The "wait and see" approach

When something doesn't happen the way it might have happened in your previous organisation, your gut instinct might be to spring into action and try to "fix the problem". It's so tempting to rush into a situation and provide everyone with a list of your solutions, but while you might have the best of intentions, it could end up backfiring on you! Often, the best thing to do is to sit back and observe.

Don't mistake this for laziness (or inefficiency), rather, it's a way to understand the full picture before making any hasty changes. You might prefer to do your own form of onboarding in the early days: sit in on meetings, observe discussions, participate in processes that are already in place and take your own notes about the team dynamics you see in person.

For large teams made up of different groups, this approach of observation vs immersion can help you find your feet more quickly. However, to the team you're joining, it may feel as though you aren't fully engaged or interested in them as individuals, so to counter this, consider setting the scene by simply letting the team know that you'll be observing and learning as you settle in.

Inheriting an established team

Your People Manager role might be new, but the team you're joining might not be. An established team, broadly speaking, is an existing or ongoing project team or group of people within the business who have worked together for a while. Certain dynamics and relationships (not to mention habits and behaviours) will pre-exist when you join a team like this.

In this scenario, you're the "new" member, but that doesn't automatically mean that you have to adopt the team's existing approaches or those of your predecessor (if there was one). There are several ways to test the water and understand how this team works together. You may, of course, learn that what looks like a functioning and smooth-running team is everything but - we didn't say this would necessarily be easy! Don't panic, though, there are several approaches to finding out:

- Participate in as many meetings with the team as possible and listen to what people are saying. Simply observe the dynamics at work in the team. In this instance, it would be advisable to let the team know that you're doing this; you can avoid nasty surprises or team members thinking that they're being judged, which is not a good foot to start on!
- Meet people and work out "who's who" within the team. Aim to find out as much as you can about how the team functions: Who's really engaged with the business or project? Who's disengaged or doesn't feel able to contribute or be productive? Who's brimming with ideas and enthusiasm? Who's driving communications or productivity?

You may well discover during these conversations and observations that there are changes that could be made to benefit team members individually or as a group. But should you jump in and make suggestions, however valuable you think they are, or should you opt to hang back and try to fit in with what's already in progress? Both of these approaches have obvious risks as well as benefits. Before you make any decisions or changes, though, it's worth writing them down and articulating the risks and benefits. In addition to being a good exercise for you, this list is something you can discuss with the team, either in one-to-ones (especially if the changes affect only a few people) or together as a group. Be sure to ask for feedback or opinions.

Your team may have insight about what changes will work, and even if they're reticent to implement those changes, having the opportunity to discuss your ideas will create an open channel of communication, which is something that's crucial for going forward.

A remote team

As you walk into the office each morning, you probably quickly greet your team as you arrive, perhaps asking them how things are going. This simple interaction is easily done, and it's something you take for granted in dealing with onsite teams.

As we mentioned earlier, getting to know your team and building a rapport with them is an important part of building relationships and trust. However, with remote workers, this task can be a bit more challenging - you can't exactly greet them in person as you walk into the building. So how do you get to know people on your team who work thousands of miles away?

Encourage sharing

The modern workplace is quite different from the one our grandparents might have recognised. For one, many modern offices are open plan, and we spend the majority of our time hunched over a computer. The idea of working remotely - and doing so successfully - wouldn't have been a reality 50 years ago! Although tools such as Slack, Skype and Google Hangouts let us quickly communicate with people half a world away, in reality, there's still a virtual "wall" between us and the people on the other end of the line. The subtleties that you can pick up on in a face-to-face conversation can often be lost over the line. This is why it's important to ensure that everyone involved, whether local or remote, is able to easily share what's going on in their world.

Consider building a channel that allows the team to share birthdays, important events or other interesting things that are happening both onsite and remotely. A regular or even daily sync call could help bring remote team members together, letting them see and speak to each other in a team environment about project progress, relevant business and team information or just to check in with how everyone's doing.

As a manager, one of the best things you can do is to build a rapport with your team, and whether they're remote or local, it's good to encourage them to build a rapport with each other, too. This is especially important if they're a newly formed team that works remotely.

Keep in mind what it feels like to be remote

As a local team or manager, it can be easy to focus on how the virtual distance is challenging for you in your own situation, but for remote workers, that distance can be tough, too. On the flip side, it's worth remembering that remote workers are passionate about their work and want to deliver successful projects just as much as you do!

It can be easy to forget about people you don't see every day or communicate with constantly. If there's an important meeting, and you fail to include them or fail to include a way for them to be online, the remote worker can feel very alienated. Of course, it isn't a deliberate action on your part, and there are plenty of ways that you can minimise the effect of this impact.

Invest in good equipment

Clear communication is vital to achieving success as a team, and in the spirit of avoiding added irritation, it's worth investing in decent equipment both for local and remote team members. Is the network connection in the office good enough? Is the audio output of decent quality? Is there a machine always available to dial into? Talk to your remote team and find out if there's anything else they need to improve communication. If they need an upgrade, for example, send them a decent headset or webcam - it can make a big difference in bridging that virtual gap.

Depending on the size of your organisation, it may seem like an added expense to invest in equipment, but we cannot stress enough how important it is. The small amount of money that you spend on equipment will save hours of lost time with dropped connections and poor audio/video, not to mention the frustration!

Harness new technology

We've heard stories of onsite teams streaming a live webcam of the office, and while this may seem a little excessive, it gives you a good idea of the kind of outside-of-the-box thinking that you can explore.

Why not see if innovative new technology can help? A robot camera called Double[3] can be controlled remotely, letting you move it around the room so people can see your face on the screen. Even if you have team members in different locations, meetings or syncs can still be achieved where all team members are present!

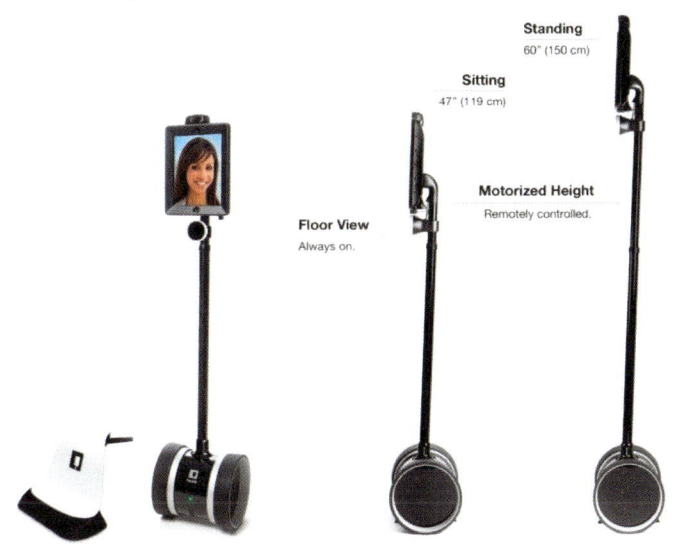

Figure 3.2 Consider using technology to your advantage when working with remote teams.

We have to admit that it's a little strange to sit in an office and see a robot driving around, but the benefit of seeing someone's face while you talk to them cannot be underestimated. This might be out of your budgetary scope, but it's good to know that technology like this exists for trying to bridge the remote communication gap.

The importance of the one-to-one

As a manager, understanding the value and importance of effective one-to-one meetings is essential to your success. One-to-ones (also known as one-on-ones, 1:1s and 1-1s) are the best opportunity you have to build rapport with your direct reports, to learn first-hand what motivates, inspires, frustrates or even angers them. Although the one-on-one meeting helps you as a manager, it's also incredibly important for your team's development and job satisfaction. In fact, done well, one-to-one meetings can inspire team members' motivation, confidence, loyalty and productivity.

Andy Grove, former CEO and cofounder of Intel, says this about one-to-ones[4]:

> *"90 minutes of your time can enhance the quality of your subordinate's work for 2 weeks, or for some 80+ hours".*

Big claim? Possibly so, but if you're willing to put in the time and effort early on, you'll see the benefits quicker than you think! It's infinitely preferable to learn about small problems early enough to help remedy them than it is to be surprised or hit by a much larger issue that has grown and festered over time.

Why bother with yet another meeting?

One-to-ones aren't just "another meeting". Without meaning to state the obvious, they're for you and your report - that's it. No group chat, no senior leader listening in, no rambling technical discussion, just the two of you meeting up with the aim of inspiring confidence and trust between you. This chat/meeting/discussion is a focal point for coaching and mentoring, sharing feedback, discussing personal issues affecting productivity and even for letting off steam. What it shouldn't feel like is a long-winded, uninteresting game of chess.

The one-to-one goes beyond a manager's "open door" policy, although as a manager, you *should* be available to your reports whenever they might need to talk to you (within reason, of course). Setting up meetings on a regular basis - more on this later - sets aside dedicated time for you and your reports to connect. A recurring diary date ensures that feedback and discussion happen regularly, that difficult issues/problems aren't allowed to build up or get worse in the interim period.

These meetings should be informal and held in a relaxed environment. We find that the best one-to-one meetings aren't long - 30 minutes or so should suffice. Depending on how the meeting goes, it could take only 15 minutes or extend slightly past the 30 minutes - it's really up to the employee. Remember that this is a chance for your direct report to get everything off their chest. As a manager, you should be doing more listening than talking here.

Accordingly, a one-to-one meeting *shouldn't* be a project progress update - those kinds of status reports are better suited to more generic team meetings, sent via email or talked over during presentations. Discussions that lean toward that kind of update should be parked or better still, taken off the agenda before the conversation begins. While we're talking about what the one-to-one shouldn't be, take great care not to turn the meeting into a therapy session for yourself as a manager! Open and honest conversation will take place where you're bound to express your own opinions or cite experiences that you've had, but don't allow yourself to take over. This one-to-one is about your report - you should have **your** own version with **your** own manager to talk about **yourself!** It seems obvious, but it's an easy thing to express your own opinions...believe us, we've been there!

Jo Says

I always open my one-to-one discussions with the same question: "How are you?" It's not meant to be a leading or even an empty question, I genuinely want to know the answer. My report can either respond with a quick "fine" or take the opportunity to share their mood, their feelings or get something off their chest. I use this question to put the person first - not their job, their project, their wins/failures or the business we both work for.

Our one-to-one is about them. Over the years, I've become quite good at reading between the lines or realising when someone says they're "fine" when they really aren't. But here's the thing: don't ask this question if you aren't going to listen to the answer! Having someone tell you how they're feeling and then changing the subject or glossing over their response will not build rapport or gain you any respect.

Our tips for setting up successful one-to-ones

By this point, the entire concept of a one-to-one might seem a little scary, but in fact they're quite easy to set up and maintain.

Set a recurring schedule

Having a regular diary date for these meetings makes sure that they're consistent and that you and your report commits to them. Having a regular one-to-one maximises effectiveness, too. Allow sufficient time to encourage interesting conversations to take place without being rushed. Choose a venue that's informal, if possible - a nearby coffee shop, a small meeting room or a quiet area in a communal place where your conversation can't be overheard are some great examples. The recurrence of one-to-ones depends on your project timeline or business model, but generally speaking, they shouldn't be so far apart that you both forget what was discussed in the previous one. They also shouldn't be so close together that there's nothing new to talk about. We tend to schedule them every two weeks or so. Remember, if either of you needs to cancel, it's better to reschedule right away to maintain the momentum and value of the regular discussion.

Have the right mindset

Put yourself in the background and allow the employee to be the focus of the conversation. Close your laptop, switch off your phone (or at the very least don't be tempted to glance at it every so often!) and give your report the respect of your attention. Unless you have specific feedback to give, try and allow the meeting to be informal and free of an agenda.

Be prepared and set the tone

If your report has already sent questions ahead or raised issues for discussion, have the relevant information at hand. Otherwise, allow them to steer the direction of the meeting and be open to what they want to discuss. If your team member is particularly quiet or seems uncomfortable, as Jo suggests above, a simple "How are you?" is a good way to start. Be open and relaxed, and let your report know that no topic is off limits as long as it's important to the employee or the manager.

Listen!

Active listening is an acquired skill. You aren't in the one-to-one conversation simply to be polite, you're showing that you respect and understand the perspective of your direct reports by giving them time to share their issues, news, objectives or feedback with you. For the team members who are less confident to take the lead in a one-to-one conversation, you can ask open-ended questions, like:

"That's interesting, can you give me an example?"

"How did that make you feel?"

"What could be a possible reason behind that?"

"What are your thoughts on how that played out?"

"If you could change the outcome, what would you change?"

Look out for body language that might indicate something not being said. Don't be tempted to fill silence gaps with chatter - give your report time to think about answers to your questions without feeling pressured.

Be prepared to discuss various topics

Through these discussions with your employees, you can get a better insight into a whole host of topics as well as find out how happy or motivated they are in their current role (think job satisfaction). You can also use them as an opportunity to dig into any areas of unhappiness or frustration, to help the person work out actions or solutions. Career development can be an ongoing topic, with one-to-one discussions being an opportunity to review progress and objectives against goals. Feedback on behaviour and current performance can be a useful discussion to have, as well as collaboration with other team members and of course feedback on you as a manager! Tempting as it might be to prepare your own agenda with lists of questions about these topics, remember that the one-to-one is about the employee - you shouldn't bombard them with direct questions that you think you need to know the answers to.

We also feel quite strongly that one-to-ones aren't an opportunity for reports to give you, their manager, a shopping list of actions they want taken or problems they want resolved. Of course, you're there to help with resolutions, but as a manager, it's far better to coach and enable someone to take the relevant or necessary actions themselves, rather than to expect you to do it all for them. How will they learn and grow in their roles otherwise? (Plus, you'll end up being overwhelmed with action items.)

Know how to wrap it up

As the one-to-one comes to an end, try to verbally summarise what you've discussed and where necessary, make action notes with your report that can be followed up on. If actions need to be taken by either party, agree when you'll review progress and what that might look like. Especially if you have a number of reports, it's a good idea to take notes of your discussion for your own benefit - it'll help jog your memory for the next meeting, too. Remember not to leave these lying around as they are a summary of a confidential conversation. Every so often, you might want to end the discussion by asking your report if it was a useful meeting, or if there's something you could do differently next time to improve it.

This is all great feedback for improving your own performance and success as a Manager.

What comes next?

It's no surprise that this chapter is the longest of the book. To learn about your new team and build a productive and friendly working relationship with them is a big challenge. If done well, it's also a great achievement, and you'll see the fruits of your labours almost immediately.

Understanding the dynamics of your team, their requirements from you and their expectations of the management process - as well as establishing a framework for good, regular communication - takes time. During the 12th century, a French proverb summed it up nicely:

> *"Rome ne s'est pas faite en un jour".*

Even in 2019, we need to realise how true this still rings: Rome wasn't built in a day! Take the ideas you've read here and implement any or all that appeal to you. Talk. Listen. Inspect. Adapt. Repeat. Create a framework that not only works for you but that enables your reports to have an open, honest and respectful relationship with you. As you nurture the rapport you build with your team, it'll blossom and grow.

If you can build strong one-to-one relationships with your reports, you'll definitely reap what you sow.

From this great starting point, you can move on to the next stage of the People Manager role, that of performance management. The next chapter helps you learn how to create development plans, objectives and goals for your reports. As part of this, your role will focus on helping your team grow their career within the business, setting out action points and goals for personal development. You'll also learn how to give feedback (both good and bad) and understand the challenges you might face when the going isn't so good.

Summary

- One of the most important things you can do as a People Manager is to build rapport with your new team. They're your greatest asset!
- The People Manager loop is a practical way to build a continuous process with management activities and responsibilities. Don't be overwhelmed - good foundations build strong houses!
- Separating key discussions into timely cadences throughout the year means you have a framework for management that will help with team communication, setting expectations for how you'll operate as their manager.
- Teams come in all shapes and sizes, so understanding how they operate will help you carry out your role more effectively.
- One-to-ones are a great tool for employee development and supporting your overall team management process. The sessions allow you to check in on motivation and morale, *and* help you and your reports get to know each other better. If you can succeed at these, your team members will feel engaged, respected and valued.

Resources

1. World Health Organisation - *Global strategy on occupational health for all: The way to health at work* - https://www.who.int/occupational_health/publications/globstrategy/en/index2.html
2. Cornell Chronicle - *"Groups that eat together perform better together"* http://news.cornell.edu/stories/2015/11/groups-eat-together-perform-better-together
3. Double Robotics - https://www.doublerobotics.com/
4. *High Output Management* - Andy Grove - Vintage 1995

PERFORMANCE MANAGEMENT

Chapter 4

*L*et's assume that you're in a good place: your team is responding well to your leadership, you're seeing great results and people seem motivated and enthusiastic at work. You feel like this is definitely #thejobforyou - you've learned new skills, tried different approaches, coached and encouraged your direct reports, and everything has worked out well so far. Job done? Inwardly smile and keep doing the same thing - if it's worked once, it'll surely keep working? Possibly yes. But what if you could improve your performance to date and see even better results going forward? You're pleased with how your team have responded to you as their new manager and the changes and improvements they've made to get to this point. What if you shared that with them?

As we've already discussed, being a People Manager is about you AND your team - communication, motivation, encouragement, risk-taking, productivity and results are undertaken, delivered and achieved together. The best way to share the feel-good factor is by praising, by giving positive feedback to those who have helped achieve it.

The power of praise

Praise is the expression of approval or admiration for someone or something. It might seem as though giving praise is a perfectly easy and natural thing to do. Something good happens or goes well, so you immediately acknowledge it, maybe through a round of applause, a high five, a smile, a belly laugh, perhaps even a whoop or holler! But what if the work, task, action or achievement isn't immediately visible? It can be difficult to remember the good things that take place over time or during a project, which means they tend to be forgotten or taken for granted by the time the end result is achieved.

It's important to be able to deliver praise in a genuine and authentic way. Continuous, sycophantic praise becomes insincere to the point where the recipient probably doesn't even hear it anymore (or listens and eye-rolls simultaneously!). At the other extreme, making an assumption that people know that they've done something good without actually telling them promotes a culture of resentment, where no one feels appreciated no matter how hard they try.

In business, we don't succeed on our own, an island cut off by the tide. We work, collaborate and integrate with other people, either with direct reports or with those people working on different teams and project groups. Every interaction we have with workmates has an effect on our day-to-day morale and motivation, even if we don't always recognise it. How many times have you finished a meeting or a discussion with a colleague and felt either demotivated and low or, conversely, brimming with enthusiasm and good will? How we behave and act around each other in the working environment has a positive or negative effect through both the words we do and don't say. But how do you know when to give praise? Here are a few scenarios with opportunities to praise team members:

One-to-one discussions

A regular one-to-one discussion with your direct report is a perfect opportunity to acknowledge good performance. By showing that you've seen good work or even improved behaviours or characteristics tells your report that you're paying attention. Maybe you can ask them how they think they're doing - some people aren't comfortable boasting about their own achievements, so teasing it out of them with your own praise and acknowledgment could boost their confidence. Have examples at hand to illustrate this - it'll give your report clear feedback on how they can build upon their strengths going forward.

Ad hoc/impromptu team situations

Nothing feels as good as getting a pat on the back in front of other people. If you hear a good comment, notice a positive contribution or see something brilliant happening in a team scenario, call it out there and then - give praise where praise is due as soon as you feel the need, don't wait and try to remember it later. Public praise can boost the morale of the team in general, despite the praise being directed at only one or two people. Along the same theme, why not send a quick email when you see or hear something being done well? Praise "in writing" might make someone's day!

Appraisals

Monthly, quarterly and annual appraisals are a more formal opportunity to give praise to your reports. If you have regular one-to-ones with your team, you'll be able to build up a story over time of their achievements. They'll also be able to regularly articulate things that have gone well with their roles, and if you aren't aware of what they consider "personal goals", it's a good chance to learn about and acknowledge them at the same time. In this scenario, the praise is of a more formal kind that can be recorded and factored into personal and career development, as well as into bonus or salary negotiations. Some businesses facilitate a process of feedback where team colleagues, other leaders and customers are polled. Being able to provide good feedback from external sources has great impact!

Celebrating the small things

Think about your own career - can you recall a time when you were praised for something you did well? How did it make you feel, and what did you think about the manager who praised you? It's unlikely that you shrugged it off and didn't feel even a tiny bit of pride in yourself! People Managers have the auspicious power to influence the way people feel and behave. Given the choice of easily boosting the morale of those we work with versus criticising and dismissing their efforts, which would you choose?

It's all part of effective and positive coaching, motivating and influencing - the attributes that make up a truly great People Manager and leader. Praising at work is an important tool for building strong relationships. Caring and appreciating your team members builds trust and loyalty.

Teams who respect, acknowledge and praise each other are far more likely to succeed than those who don't. As Maya Angelou once said[1]:

> *"I've learned that people will forget what you said, people will forget what you did, but people will never forget how you made them feel".*

Praise is obviously a great tool for boosting self-esteem - in fact, it's the natural choice for recognising good work. But what about how it helps stalled career development or the way it reignites a demotivated employee? Those team members who seem to blend into the background, overshadowed by the "shining stars" of the group, will quickly assume that their contribution is somehow inferior if no one notices what they're doing, too. This is where carefully chosen words of praise can make a big difference. The important thing to remember is that you shouldn't wait for a significant achievement to praise these individuals. As their manager, you'll know how they're progressing in their role. You'll have insight into the challenges or difficulties they face, even into the problems that they've had negative feedback about. Linking praise to their improvement plan or objectives helps them quickly see how they're making a difference and recognise what "good" looks like for their role. It's a fast, positive feedback loop: make an improvement - receive praise or recognition - feel motivated to do more.

Note that this doesn't mean you should make insignificant comments! Giving praise in a subtle, unobtrusive way can often be the secret motivator for employees who aren't used to having their work recognised. Giving a small example of why you're giving praise is useful, too.

For example:

Praise: "The way you worded that report was spot on".
Why: *"The execs liked the level of detail"*.

Praise: "I appreciated how you looked after the new starter this week".
Why: *"It really helped them get up to speed quickly"*.

Praise: "You worked hard to finish that feature on time last week".
Why: *"It meant we didn't slip our deliverable date"*.

By following this simple format for giving praise, your feedback will be more sincere and tangible - the recipient knows that their work has been noticed and, more importantly, *why*, which can help them improve and aim to replicate their behaviour.

It's always a good idea to give praise quickly, when you recognise or notice the good work being done! Be quicker to praise than you are to criticise, and you'll become a motivating and credible manager.

Jo Says

It's often a surprise (albeit a nice one!) to get good feedback...especially if you're a manager. After all, it's your job to praise your team, not theirs to praise you. In my case, I had to facilitate a particularly tricky meeting because my team members were behaving unprofessionally with each other, and the situation needed to be addressed immediately. I quickly planned the feedback session, making sure that the focus was on the impact of their behaviour (rather than the reason behind it).

Although it was uncomfortable at times for the attendees, the meeting ended with everyone agreeing to do better going forward. Afterward, I received not one but two emails from participants, noting what a positive and well-handled meeting it was. This made me feel great! I had taken a negative, potentially damaging situation and through feedback and examples, was able to help the team understand their impact and turn things around. To get praise for doing this made me really respect my team and made a difficult situation a lot easier to prevent happening again.

Praise and personal growth

One of your goals as a People Manager is to ensure that your reports are engaged and happy. With a few simple changes, encouraging employee engagement can be done in many ways, for example, through:

- emphasis on work/life balance at your company
- good, positive office environment
- team building events
- Friday night outings

According to Chester Elton (speaker, motivational expert and co-author of the best-selling management book, *The Carrot Principle*)[2]:

> *"The number one driver of engagement is opportunity and well-being. The number one driver of opportunity and well-being is recognition and appreciation…you don't just want employees satisfied, you want them engaged, because an engaged employee gives you their discretionary efforts".*

Lack of engagement due to lack of appreciation can be a cause of conflict in the workplace, be it between team members or between you and your reports. Do you know what motivates your team to come to work or to do their best? Money might be the most obvious answer, but not everyone is motivated solely by cash - there are plenty of people who might have plenty of money (by our standards!) but still choose to show up. Positive motivation tends to be the driver here (the carrot), the type of push that encourages someone to succeed if they expect a reward.

Receiving praise or recognition is definitely a reward in this case, and it can be as simple as acknowledging an achievement, a success, a personal challenge completed or a goal reached.

Negative motivation, on the other hand, is about punishment, the fear of the consequence of not achieving an intended goal. For some people, it can be effective - the consequence of not doing something drives them harder to succeed (the stick). Of course, the combination of carrot and stick can work in many scenarios, but most of us would rather reward people with carrots than keep after them with sticks.

Motivation and personal growth go hand in hand with positive praise and recognition. Surely, you can think of times in your own career when you received great feedback that spurred you on to greater productivity. Knowing that you're doing something well boosts your self-confidence and self-esteem, both of which help your personal growth and improvement.

The process of giving feedback

As a People Manager, you have the power to give constructive feedback in a number of scenarios:

- regular one-to-one meetings with reports
- formal appraisals and performance reviews
- project reviews and retrospectives
- difficult workplace situations or conflicts
- personal development and career coaching sessions

Even the most self-aware person can't possibly measure or rate their effectiveness in isolation. Our job as managers is to help make our teams and the business successful, and to do that, we have to regularly connect and work on ways to make continuous improvement. Effective feedback celebrates successes but also calls out areas where things aren't going to plan; it gives insight and direction to help the recipient turn things around.

Perhaps one of the most important things to do before attempting to deliver any kind of feedback is to ask the intended recipient if they're open to receiving it. We shouldn't always assume that our teams are ready and willing to hear what we think, so it might be more appropriate to schedule a specific meeting for it or be prepared to discuss feedback in a different way. Of course, if a team member says they don't want any feedback, that's a different issue; Chapter 5 offers some tips.

Feedback "no no's"

From our own experience of getting things wrong and improving the way we deliver feedback, here are some tips for what *not* to do when starting the conversation:

✗ "Everyone thinks you are/you should…"
This isn't a helpful way to open a conversation about feedback. You're about to deliver your feedback, regardless of who else had input to it. Making the recipient feel embarrassed or inferior by suggesting that their whole team feels they're doing something wrong is not the purpose or the desired outcome of this conversation.

✗ "If I were you, I would…"
Put simply, you are not them! Everyone is an individual, and the way they behave, conduct themselves or make their own choices are personal and driven by their own decisions and attributes. Feedback discussions shouldn't be treated as an opportunity to encourage everyone to behave in the same way or to be a carbon copy of you!

✗ "You always…"
Rarely is this phrase true. Although we might see certain actions or behaviours occur quite frequently, they're unlikely to be constantly repeated. The feedback you're giving is intended to give the recipient a chance to boost their performance and improve their skills, so making them feel that they make the same mistakes every time is likely to demotivate them and overshadow the constructive nature of the feedback process.

❌ **"I've heard through the grapevine..." or "Rumour has it..."**
This is such a poor way to open a feedback conversation! As a manager, you should adopt a confident, assured and trustworthy tone. Giving the person the impression that you listen to and believe workplace gossip or throwaway comments will make them feel picked on and will break any trust you've built up. Feedback should only be shared when it is well-observed (by you) and has examples to back it up.

❌ **"I notice that you... [invokes the feedback sandwich]"**
Although this method tends to be recommended for new managers as a gentler way to deliver negative feedback, it can be counterproductive. The premise is that the manager layers examples of good feedback on either side of corrective or more negative feedback. However, when on the receiving end of this mixed bag, it's easy to ignore all the positives once you hear something less likeable - that's human nature! The recipient is therefore confused about the purpose of the feedback and potentially unsure of which is more important to you, giving the entire session little value. It also undermines your respect as a manager - the purpose of the "sandwich" model is to make the process more comfortable for *you*, when in reality, your role is to support and coach your reports.

By avoiding these phrases, you'll come across as a strong and supportive leader, not a smug and superior boss.

The *BEER* model of giving feedback

Giving negative (albeit constructive) feedback is one of the hardest roles of being an effective People Manager - it can be uncomfortable, and you can't predict how the recipient will react. One way to conquer this uncertainty is to use the BEER feedback model, where BEER stands for behaviour, effect, expectation and result. To avoid an awkward or unfocused discussion, this tried-and-tested method gives a framework for linking your observations to the impact of certain behaviours (or lack thereof).

Let's take an example of a team member who makes frequent assumptions that they're right and dismisses other opinions or ignores colleagues in meetings and workplace discussions. Once you've asked if you can give them some feedback, and they have agreed, you can start:

***B**ehaviour* - outline the unfavourable or problematic behaviour that you've observed. Keep it factual and focused.

"At times, your attitude comes across as patronising and dismissive of what your colleagues are trying to contribute".

***E**ffect* - demonstrate what effects this behaviour has, be it on other people, productivity, projects, etc.

"It's preventing healthy collaboration because your colleagues feel like their opinions are not valued. They're becoming reluctant to contribute, which is affecting productivity".

***E**xpectation* - state what it is that you would like your team member to do about this feedback, what they can do to indicate improvement.

"I'd like you to think about how you can adapt the way in which you interact with your teammates and how you can be more open and willing to engage with different ideas and opinions. Let's meet again in a few weeks to review how you're getting on".

***R**esult* - describe the change this feedback will bring about and articulate the improvements you would like to see.

"By being more mindful of the way you interact with others, by improving your willingness to collaborate with your team, we'll be able to work more harmoniously and productively as a team".

The premise behind this model is that you keep your personal opinions out of the discussion. You're making it clear for the recipient what the issue is, how they can/should change and what improvements such changes will bring about. Having examples of the behaviour enables them to understand the impact of their actions, and the result shows what can be achieved if they accept the feedback. You're supporting their ability to make changes without criticising them, being factual without adding your opinion and coaching to give them the opportunity for personal growth.

Armed with these tips, tools and tested methods, you should feel a whole lot more confident about giving feedback. Remember, the purpose of giving it is to acknowledge and praise or to dissuade negative or counterproductive behaviours. Ensuring that you have examples of either allows you to deliver the feedback objectively, making it more valuable and constructive for the recipient.

Creating performance plans

We talked earlier about the People Manager loop, the cadences throughout the year where formal and informal discussions happen with your employees. By now, you've got your one-to-ones organised and happening regularly, and you're using feedback to help shape your team's behaviours and productivity. So why do you need to think about performance plans? In a nutshell, performance plans tie all these other tools and processes together. A good plan provides a solid foundation for ongoing discussion, performance review and assessment and a constant reference point for measuring progress.

Most businesses will have an HR expectation of formal performance plans. These plans can come in different guises, from simply setting up objectives to articulating goals at a personal or team/business level.

Importantly, a performance plan is a *documented* process, a recorded agreement between employee and manager. Ideally (and in our experience), a performance plan is usually discussed and agreed upon at the beginning of a development cycle. This may be the start of the financial/business year, the commencement of a new project or a new hire beginning their new role. Before you wonder how you're going to set goals for all your new reports, remember a key factor: a performance plan is a collaborative process that begins with discussion to articulate and agree on some specific objectives.

Goals

What is the expected deliverable or output? This gives the goals structure and your report a clear deliverable to aim for. Clarity is important here.

Method

How are you going to get there? This is where collaboration comes into the process - you can discuss which behaviours need to change, any new skills that can be learned, tools that can be used and knowledge that can be gained from you or other colleagues.

Definition of "done"

How will you know that you've achieved your goals? Does the plan need check-in points along the way to review progress? Set out a method to obtain feedback so that your report knows whether they're on track to achieve their goals.

What kind of goals should be included?

Your reports should be encouraged to think about what they would like to achieve in the period covered by the performance plan. As their manager, your job is to offer guidance, steering them toward important aspects of their personal or career development (using feedback highlighting areas of weakness or opportunities for growth). They should feel confident enough to set goals or objectives that they feel are realistic to achieve.

They may have more personal goals they want to aim for, such as becoming more confident delivering presentations or mastering a particular software package, but just as important are the goals relevant to your team or the wider business, such as finishing "xyz project" by the required deadline or ensuring that a specific sales target is reached.

Although we would recommend that most of an employee's goals should be realistic (because what's the point in starting a cycle with impossible objectives?), it's often good practise to include one or two "stretch goals". These outcomes or deliverables would be great to achieve but either aren't a main priority or have too many restrictive factors, like funding, resources or time. But if your report wants to have something extra to aim for and is motivated to achieve it, why not? It's important to note that a stretch goal shouldn't be prioritised over core performance plan goals - those should always be the most important because they're relevant now!

How do you measure progress toward goals?

Once your reports have set their goals and objectives for the cycle (with your guidance and sign-off, of course), is the job done? Nope! How are you going to know whether your team members are on track, miles adrift or struggling to make progress? This is where one-to-ones become useful. Goals can be flexible: if something is proving too difficult or perhaps no longer relevant to the employee, the project or the business, it should be adjusted or removed. One-to-one discussions enable you to check in with your reports and encourage them to share progress about objectives, keeping goals on the front burner and not pushing them to the back of the priority queue!

Dean Says

In our careers as People Managers, we've always created goals for the calendar year. These goals can cover an entire year if they're long-term and need progress over time or sustained learning. We regularly monitor the goals of our team each quarter, setting aside specific one-to-one time to discuss progress, problems or achievements. Goals that have been achieved each quarter can be demonstrated before being marked as "completed". This is a good way to show regular improvement, either in personal development or in project success. It also keeps the process relevant and focused, which ultimately is more meaningful for your team members' performance and trackable for you as their manager.

How to continuously develop your reports

Goal setting - and the discussions around progressing toward goals and ideally reaching them - is the framework for a healthy development trajectory within roles and career paths. Achieving goals not only gives team members a great sense of accomplishment (and hopefully pride!), but it's the manifestation of learning new skills and pushing the boundaries of confidence and abilities. So why stop there? When something is good, why not make it even better? Encourage and motivate your reports to try and achieve more, either by adopting new skills or improving the ones they already have.

You can't do this for them, but as their manager, you can coach or provide support and guidance for them to keep learning and developing.

70:20:10: a model for continuous learning

The idea behind the 70:20:10[3] model shown in Figure 4.1 is that the majority of our learning - approximately 70% - comes through experience, literally via on-the-job activities and informal learning opportunities. Roughly 20% tends to come from social interaction with colleagues, be it workplace colleagues, networking opportunities or discussions with friends and like-minded people. Only the remaining 10% will come as a result of formal learning such as training courses, documentation, online classes or physical classrooms.

Figure 4.1 70:20:10 is a model for continuous learning.

Using this 70:20:10 model can be an empowering way to encourage your reports to expand their knowledge and abilities. Of course, your business can provide access to a whole array of formal training sessions, workshops and professional courses, but why not let your reports decide for themselves what suits their appetite for personal development? Let them tailor their learning through their own on-the-job experiences to find areas that they want to focus on or learn more about.

David Robertson, the VP EMEA The Forum Corporation, says the following[4]:

> *"What 70:20:10 tells us is that learning is a continuous act that never stops. That it takes place in different arenas, some that we set up, some that we just happen to work in. You can help to move your culture away from a situation where people just turn up to a training event not knowing what they're doing or why they're there".*

Collaborative learning allows team members to progress beyond what they would have been able to learn alone by sharing achievements, learning new methods, discussing risks and results and simply observing the thought processes of others. If your team works in the agile project management process, for example, there are multiple opportunities to work collaboratively together. This is possible in project-planning sessions, mid-project "show and tell" sessions, end-of-project reviews and retrospective workshops to look back on a project's good and bad points. You'll also find that sharing knowledge, insights and opinions happens in a far more informal way at lunch, at a cafe over a quick coffee or at the gym after work. Everything is a learning opportunity!

Despite making up only 10% of the formula, formal learning can be the backbone of any learning experience. After all, if you want to learn to drive, you can't (and shouldn't) sit behind the wheel and simply be "let loose" on the main roads after talking about it with your friends! Formal tuition is required, along with learning the rules and theory; once learned, all of this knowledge can support your practical experience and help you become a competent and confident (not to mention legal) driver. The same is true for career training. You may want to offer or mandate training courses or workshops, provided either onsite by your business or offsite by reputable suppliers. Your reports might want to aim for professional accreditation or achieve certificates for their learning. These types of learning opportunities will enable your employees to achieve vocational, professional or regulatory standards, which will go on to be further enhanced and improved by informal, collaborative and on-the-job exponential learning.

Summary

- When things are going well, it's always good to celebrate and acknowledge that fact. Feedback can increase confidence and encourage employees to continue at that level of performance.
- Feedback is an essential tool for People Managers - praising the good stuff and correcting the not-so-good stuff ensures that team members understand what is expected of them and see that you're an attentive manager who values them.
- Finding a feedback method that works for you is a personal choice, but the most important objective is to provide examples to accompany your feedback - this enables you to deliver observations that are prejudice-free and unbiased.
- Don't get fooled into serving up a feedback sandwich! Instead, be clear, be fair and be focused.
- Be quick to praise and slow to blame.
- Performance plans are a great framework for creating and measuring progress toward development goals. They also encourage useful and focused communication between People Managers and their reports.
- Continuous learning is achievable by everyone on your team (including you!). Iterate on what's going well and fix the things that aren't.
- Formal training + collaborative learning + on-the-job experience = continuous development for your reports.

References

1. *Maya Angelou Quotes* - The Guardian - https://www.theguardian.com/books/2014/may/28/maya-angelou-in-fifteen-quotes
2. *The Carrot Principle* by Chester Elton - Simon & Schuster UK - 2009
3. *70/20/10 Model (Learning and Development)* - Wikipedia - https://en.wikipedia.org/wiki/70/20/10_Model_(Learning_and_Development)
4. *70:20:10 – A Model Approach for Learning?* - Personnel Today - https://www.personneltoday.com/hr/702010-a-model-approach-for-learning

Chapter

ROUGH SEAS AHEAD

*L*et's face it, regardless of how smoothly things start off on your journey as a People Manager, eventually you'll face some bumps in the road. As we've mentioned throughout this book, humans are complex creatures, there's no cheat sheet for dealing with our history, cultures and personalities - simply put, everyone's different!

In this chapter, we'll take a closer look at some approaches to dealing with conflict in the workplace. Poor performance of employees can also lead to difficult conversations, often making formal performance plans necessary. We'll also explore some of our own techniques for dealing with these situations and the difficult conversations that you may need to have at some point.

Before we start, these words might help you reframe your thoughts if you're faced with a difficult situation:

> *When something bad happens, you have three choices. You can let it define you, destroy you, or strengthen you.*

Our aim is to help you become stronger!

Dealing with conflict

As much as we hate admitting it, there comes a time when all People Managers face conflict. Whether it's among different members of your team or between you and your team members, it is inevitable and will occur as long as humans coexist.

Cast your mind back to the last time you handled a conflict - what did it feel like? Did your heart beat faster? Perhaps your palms were sweaty, or your face was flushed? This is your body's way of preparing for *fight-or-flight* mode, a basic survival mechanism that might seem at odds with the average office environment. Your emotional reactions are a heady mixture of anger, frustration, confusion and dread, not only about the conflict itself but about the thought of facing it and dealing with the steps to resolve it.

When conflict arises in the workplace, we've noticed that people either hide away from discomfort and hope the issue dissipates or they address it head on, often without filtering the words they use. Neither of these responses are the ideal way to react. If you avoid problems, they grow and slowly become worse over time; if you rush head-first into challenging an issue, you can easily cause more damage (to yourself and to others).

At your earliest opportunity, try to schedule a meeting (chat/coffee/formal discussion) where the key issues that caused the conflict can be aired and discussed. This gives you and the other parties involved a chance to think about what actually happened, the impact and possible resolutions, which is the discussion's outcome. Come to this meeting with your thoughts organised and be ready to articulate the following steps clearly:

1. Agree on the "rules of engagement". These rules may be as simple as agreeing to allow each person to speak freely without interruption, to listen to each other, to be respectful of the language used and to avoid aggressive behaviour or personal insults. You might want an

independent third party present to help facilitate the discussion (we hesitate to say referee, but sometimes having a mediator can diffuse the strong emotions at play and also ensure that everyone gets fair time to talk and respond).

2. Try to ignore preconceptions you have of the other people involved. These assumptions are probably based on previous behaviours and circumstances or caused by the conflict itself. An agreement to have an open mind is a good start to what may seem very uncomfortable at first.

3. Agree on the conflict that you are there to resolve. This might seem obvious, but if you have differing opinions about how the issue has arisen, you won't get very far in resolving it.

4. Talk about what happened as you understand it and describe the impact it has had on you. The issue might have had an emotional or stress-related effect, or it might have impacted a project, team or deliverable. Being able to articulate the impact gives the issue real context and demonstrates the negative effect it's having.

5. Reframe and restate. Once you and the other parties involved have completed Step 4, ask each other questions to further understand the issue or clarify what has been said.

6. Discuss what conflict resolution looks like. This point of the conversation can be seen as the "second half": the issues have been raised, the impacts described and understood (or at least acknowledged). Now it's time to focus on a resolution, solution or outcome. What changes would you like to see happen? What actions need to be taken to get there? Is it a clear-cut outcome, or are there several options to compromise on?

7. Avoid *not* reaching a resolution. It might be tempting to give up or take a break, but you want to do everything you can to not only come up with a way to fix the problem, but also to make sure that a solution doesn't benefit only one side. If you have an obvious winner and loser, you won't promote team unity going forward, and you'll create a theme for how future conflicts might end up.

8. Attempt to end at a *collaborative* resolution. In this style of conflict management, all parties are involved in the agreed-on approach to fixing the conflict. The final outcome is accepted by everyone at the table as the best resolution.

In spite of all your best efforts, a conflict can sometimes be too damaging or deep to make a collaborative resolution possible. In this scenario, a *compromise* might be the best outcome. Each party will need to sacrifice part of their solution - no single player can win, and not all players can agree (going forward, this result could lead to resentment among those involved). To reach a compromise, part of the problem may have to be left out or the resolution "downgraded" so that the outcome is less than ideal. However, if this is the only option, you may decide that it's the best way forward. Ultimately, the conflict will have been resolved and lessons learned to prevent it recurring.

Conflict among team members

There has never been an organisation in the history of the world with zero conflict among its people. But it's worth remembering that you're responsible for how the behaviour of your team is manifested and for being conscious of how it can affect others. Ignoring an issue will ultimately let it fester under the surface. The result might be that some of your best people leave, simply because you didn't nip a problem in the bud.

If you determine that speaking to the team members involved in a conflict together might work best, provide each with uninterrupted time to give their (fact-based) side of the story. Once everyone has had this opportunity, ask each of them to offer ideas on how the situation could be resolved and how all parties could move forward. It's important to hear both sides of the story first. Just because one person told you something about a series of events, don't take that as gospel.

Moreover, discussing conflict or having a difficult conversation doesn't necessarily need to lead to a formal meeting or even a public quarrel! Consider raising it in a one-to-one to get each of your direct reports' thoughts on the issue. The important thing is to address the issue as soon as it happens…if you ignore it or leave it too long, it will only leave the people involved feeling ambushed when they finally *are* confronted with the need to meet. Recent issues are also fresh in everyone's minds and can thus be discussed constructively.

Regardless of when or how you meet, always have examples of the issue you want to confront and the impact it's having.

Finally, always write up a summary of the conversation and/or solution. Whether employees like it or not, it's important that you document *all* workplace incidents. Recording these events will help you monitor behaviour over time and notice any repeat offenders who might be negatively impacting your team. Include the who, what, when, where and how, as well as the resolution that all parties agreed on and committed to uphold.

Take any form of conflict among people seriously. Having a laissez-faire attitude will always result in the problem growing and its impact being far more serious and harder to resolve down the road.

Sometimes you may learn of a conflict where your involvement is neither needed nor wanted. If it becomes clear that two people need to "slog it out" and can do so without involving others, don't get involved. Allow them the space to handle it themselves, but you should give them a directive that it has to be resolved. They are employees; this isn't a schoolyard squabble, their actions directly affect your team, and as such, they must take responsibility for those actions.

Dean Says

One of my teams had two people who really didn't like each other, and their constant quips and sarcastic comments started to get worse over time. The lack of respect for the other person was becoming obvious, and more importantly for the business, their productivity was suffering. Other team members noticed the bad atmosphere but felt unable to do anything, not knowing the cause of their apparent mutual dislike. So, because the impact of the disagreement was spreading, my only option was to speak to both parties.

I chatted to each person individually and asked what had caused the problem. Acknowledging the issue that was affecting them in a manner that was genuine was a step in the right direction. Had I laughed it off or belittled their distress, my ability to help them work things out would have been greatly reduced. I encouraged both to prepare points to share with each other in a discussion overseen by me. They both described the problem as they saw it and gave examples to show the other person how it had affected them. To cut a long (and at times uncomfortable) story short, they both apologised for letting the issue drag on for so long and agreed to work together to prevent it from happening again. We also agreed to meet later to discuss whether the agreement held. They had confidence in my support of their plan and were able to separate personal issues from professional behaviour.

Had this issue been left unaddressed for any longer, the perception would be that I supported negative behaviour, and the disrespect would have grown, unchecked.

Conflict with a direct report

Conflicts that arise with one of your own reports can be especially hard. It might be that you've had a communication breakdown, drawn incorrect conclusions about something or made assumptions that were not shared by the other party. The same mantra is as relevant here as it is when conflict happens between others: tackle it immediately, do not be tempted to ignore it. If you have a good relationship with your report, and you think that the disagreement can be resolved between the two of you (no need for a mediator), discuss the facts and allow each other time to express your points of view. Typically, just being able to express disappointment, hurt or anger diffuses the situation: your team member feels listened to and can articulate why they might feel angry, and you in turn can express your own perspective, particularly if the conflict arose over something you reacted to. Emotion will come into it, especially if the conflicting parties are upset or angry, but try to keep the discussion primarily about the facts - you may need written notes to help you give examples of behaviours or impacts.

Emotional responses may get worse before they get better - and that's okay. Upset, frustration and anger are normal if someone feels aggrieved. If nothing else, observing an emotional reaction will help each of you understand the impact that the conflict is having. Just remember to keep your responses professional: blowing your top and uttering a stream of expletives might make you feel better initially, but it will create a very different image of you as a manager!

Talking together also gives you a chance to discuss an ideal end result for both of you. You may not completely agree, and a resolution might seem out of reach initially, but breaking down the facts and discussing steps you can take to reach a compromise is the only way that you'll be able to resolve things between you. We aren't saying that all of this can or should be done in one session or discussion. Draft a plan or agenda for the first attempt to resolve the conflict and be ready to pause and digest what you've both discussed. Agree to meet again but document what your next discussion will aim to cover and try to articulate an end goal or at least an action. Continue to do this until you both feel progress is being achieved.

Of course, there may be a time when you feel that the conflict has become something bigger than you can deal with (we don't anticipate this happening very often, but it's good to be prepared). Your report might feel more comfortable discussing or even escalating their concerns to someone other than you. The severity of the conflict may mean that it has to be dealt with by a third party in your business. In this scenario, consider asking another manager or an HR facilitator to mediate your discussion. They can ensure that both parties get an equal chance to speak and should take notes for you to refer to afterward. They can also encourage you both to listen or to moderate the behaviours at play - whatever is relevant to the conflict that you're experiencing. Don't feel that you always have to resolve everything yourself if it becomes something you can't manage alone. You may be a People Manager, but being a superhero is not something that goes with the territory - everyone needs support at some point in their role.

Difficult conversations

Let's be honest - it feels good to give people good feedback. Praise where it's due can light up a person's day and put a smile on their face. But one of the hardest parts of the People Manager role is when you have to deliver bad feedback or partake in tough conversations. Many People Managers shy away from this, which can have a detrimental effect on the team in the long run. It might not show up in the first few days or weeks, but it eventually will creep in.

Imagine a world where everyone thinks everything that they've ever done is perfect and they aren't responsible for their actions - this utopia in our minds could cause utter chaos!

Yes, having tough conversations *is* tough and it's much easier to dodge and work around them. However, the long-term negative impact is no joke. The effect this avoidance can have on the entire workplace culture is massive. It may not be obvious, but your team are constantly looking to you and assessing how you react to different situations. You have a responsibility to lead by example, to set the scene for how you approach, unpick and effectively deal with challenging scenarios when strong feedback has to be delivered.

*Regardless of whether the number of people that you manage is 2 or 200, how you react during the good times **and the bad** will define the culture of the team.*

In practical terms, what does this really mean? Well, it means that whether you like it or not, your team will be influenced by your management style. For example, if you're competitive, you may find that your team will be more aggressive. If you're analytical and data-driven, this will influence your team to make metrics-based decisions. On the other hand, if you deliberate too long over decisions, your people may have a hard time moving as quickly as they should.

This is why making time as a team for honest communication is essential. It may not be easy to approach, but using a framework like the one mentioned above can go a long way. Approaching a tough conversation requires courage and determination, but in the end, it is always worth it.

Coaching or leading through tough situations

Faced with your first difficult conversation, new conflict or poor performance situation, you'll no doubt wonder what the best approach will be. Should you coach your report through the issues they're facing by giving advice, listening and offering support? Perhaps you think that putting options on the table to articulate and motivate your report toward a preferred solution is preferable? Or maybe the situation has been bubbling for a long time, without progress or improvement, and you want to put a clear plan into place to resolve it?

Discussions about coaching, leading and managing are everywhere, and many, *many* books, blogs and journals have been written about this important subject. We don't have enough pages to go into detail about these topical management styles, but hopefully the following examples will help you understand the difference between them and help you select a style that suits your needs. All will take you in the same direction, but they require different skills as a People Manager (hats that you'll have to wear at some point in your role). What is common across all of them? Communication, of course - **well-thought out**, **well-articulated** and **well-delivered communication**.

You may assume (understandably!) that being a good manager means that you'll also need to be good at coaching your reports. Is there even a difference between the two? The simple answer is yes - they require vastly different skill sets. Would you be surprised if we told you that not all good managers naturally have the skills to be good coaches? We will talk more about coaching versus mentoring later in Chapter 7, but it's worth saying now that throughout a good leader's career development, some coaching skills won't have been learned or acquired, or indeed even have been needed to deliver more traditional management practises.

Leading is about inspiring, communicating a vision to the team and beyond, steering the team or organisation to think bigger, more strategic and longer term. A company CEO will do this at the highest level of a business, but for People Managers, it can also mean helping to connect an individual's role to a broader objective or helping the team through a challenging or uncertain time or event. You're offering solutions or influencing decisions, and the element of uncertainty, ambiguity or indecisiveness is minimised with this approach. When tackling a conflict or having a difficult conversation, there's a temptation to set out how you expect the situation to be resolved when you're a manager. After all, you know better...right?

If a conflict has gone on for a while, and attempts have been made to reach a solution, or at least discuss the problems at the root, yet no progress has been made, it might be more appropriate for you to rely on your leadership skills. But rather than being directive and issuing commands for how you want things resolved, you can still lead without being overly assertive. Suggest more steps that can be taken. Ask if the parties involved would like help from you or anyone else to progress. Give an example where you've used a particular dialogue or action to bring about change. Use your leadership influence to make sure change happens, and make it clear that not making change for the better isn't an option.

Good managers give direction to the groups they manage, of course, and the willingness to exert leadership is often why they get promoted. But the most effective managers who are also effective coaches learn to be selective about giving direction. Rather than using their conversations as an opportunity to exert a strong influence, make recommendations and provide unambiguous direction, they take a step back and try to draw out the views of their talented, experienced staff.

This is where *coaching* is a valuable skill to draw on. Having good coaching skills is all about helping and enabling your reports to become more effective. Rather than telling them the answer, you empower them and help them find the solution themselves. This is done by supporting and involving your employees in the process, whilst still managing their performance to deliver results. In this situation, you gain the trust of the parties involved by listening to the reasons for the conflict and asking probing questions to get to the heart of the problem. Turn the situation around and ask them what outcome they would like to see. Encourage them to think of how to get to that outcome, down to the step by step. Ask them to think about how they'll know that they've succeeded and how they might prevent the same situation from arising in the future. Of course, you can offer ideas or use the "if I were you…" construction to get your point across, but this then becomes *your* solution. The parties concerned are unlikely to believe in the result if they didn't fully participate in reaching a resolution.

Performance improvement plans

There may be a time when one of your employees underperforms in their role. After delivering constructive feedback and communicating your expectations (and those of your business), you may have to consider a performance improvement plan (PIP). People Managers typically use a PIP to help their report improve, but if necessary, it can be coupled with disciplinary action.

We won't cover this topic in detail here, but do seek advice from your HR practitioner before proceeding down this path. Put simply, a PIP is a formal tool to assist your employees in improving their performance, so it's important for you to understand what should be included, assuming your HR representative agrees that it's the correct course of action. At the very least, a PIP should

- clearly and objectively explain why the person's work isn't of the

required standard
- give clear details about the expected improvement and provide objectives that can be easily measured (follow the same process as the goal setting outlined in Chapter 4)
- provide a time period the PIP will cover and set out how often it will be reviewed (and by whom, including sign-off responsibilities)
- give clear deliverables/goals with required-by dates and criteria for sign-off
- clarify the consequences if performance fails to improve (again, your HR representative will need to be involved here)
- specify whether any support, coaching, mentoring or training will be provided

Starting a PIP can seem scary because it's a much more formal way of engaging your reports to turn around their behaviour. We always advocate communicating closely with them first to clearly articulate the problems as you see them (starting with feedback and examples of the problems and their impact). Speaking from experience, going down the formal route with a PIP should be a last resort!

Try to discuss a way forward within a set time period during which you can coach and advise on the job to give employees the opportunity to turn things around. You may find that they're struggling to do what is required or have issues that they're finding too hard to work with. Try to remove these blockers if you can, encourage open dialogue and give clear guidance for how they can improve or move past the problems you think are impacting their development. If you've been through these steps and still see no improvement, you should discuss a more formal approach with your HR team.

Don't feel disheartened! Some problems with employees and their performance can't be resolved or improved, no matter what steps you take to support and guide them. As long as you have done what you can to approach the problem fairly and professionally, with documented steps, you can reflect on the situation and take valuable learning points from the experience.

Being liked as a manager

So far, we've talked a lot about conflict, difficult conversations and the differences between being directive and collaborative. Any of these scenarios can leave you feeling as if you're no longer on the same side as your reports, that you're the "big, bad wolf" simply because you're the person responsible for dealing with and resolving contentious issues like this. Nobody wants to feel like they're unpopular, but you can separate this from feeling the need to be liked by everyone.

Being a good People Manager doesn't mean that you can't foster or continue friendships with your team members or reports. If you have great camaraderie with a team that you've recently joined, or if you've been promoted within a team that you used to be a part of, you don't have to automatically stop these friendships at work. Instead, you may need to tweak them as your role matures and develops. But how?

First of all, recognise that there has to be a difference between being warm and friendly to your team members and being their buddy. They do need to understand that, as their manager, you're being held accountable for their work, so there will be times when you have to be directive and make decisions that not everyone will like. There will also be many more times when you have to pull together and support each other. You're managing a team, but you're still part of that team. It may seem like a difficult balance to achieve, but you can be warm and friendly, open, honest and trustworthy (after all, these are the strengths that make you a great manager).

Just be mindful of confusing your team about your role by trying to ingratiate yourself with everyone or by trying to be liked 100% of the time! It's tempting to get drawn into office gossip or watercooler rants about managers and company decisions, but you'll need to learn how to politely back off from these situations. Simply excusing yourself politely means that you won't be in the excruciatingly difficult position of "piggy in the middle", where you have to support your reports but remain loyal to your managers, the business and your new role. Set your own boundaries - maintain the level of friendship that you're comfortable with, and don't be surprised when you feel compromised or need to take a step back to deal with challenges to your management role.

What if your reports used to be your teammates?

One of the biggest (and most challenging) transitions you might face as a People Manager is if you've been promoted to manage people who were previously your peers. There's no way to conceal the fact that this shift in dynamics isn't easy: it requires you to re-establish your identity, your relationships with your team and your role within the business. It seems daunting, not to mention awkward, so how can you best face this challenge?

Start by talking to your reports, especially if you've received negative feedback or are feeling unsupported in your new role. Explain what the transition means for you (i.e., why you were selected for this role or why you wanted to take the opportunity to be a People Manager within your business). Extend an invitation to people who feel uncomfortable or challenged by you moving from colleague to manager and ask what you can do to make the transition work for them. You might want to communicate your goals and objectives with them as well. What do you want to achieve or help improve as their manager? Being open and honest is a fundamental way to demonstrate your support for team members; it also shows that you're committed to their success, the team or business's success and your own success and continuous improvement as a leader.

If at first you don't succeed?

There's an old English proverb that advises, "If at first you don't succeed, try, try again". Put simply, don't give up too easily because persistence always pays off in the end. Not everything you implement or introduce as a new People Manager will result in the outcome you anticipated or hoped for. Success is not always easy to come by, let alone as quickly as you might have planned, but becoming disillusioned and throwing in the towel isn't the solution either! At first it may seem as if your efforts have failed, but take this as an opportunity to gain some perspective on how you're feeling. As we discussed earlier, there are myriad ways to tackle difficult, challenging or simply overwhelming people problems. There's no "one size fits all" solution (sorry if that's not what you were hoping to hear). We're dealing with people here, human beings with all their complexities, nuances, personalities and mind-boggling habits. Instead of giving up, now is the time to try new ways of tackling things. Think about scenarios in different ways or adopt a different mindset to help you see the situation from a different perspective. But how?

Trying a different approach

You've been ploughing through difficult conversations, worrying about how to perform conflict resolution, and you feel like you're out of ideas for moving forward. Perhaps now is the time to think outside the box and come up with a completely different perspective? We aren't going to be patronising and suggest that "having fun" cures everything, but maybe it's worth changing things up a bit - what's to lose? Here are some ideas for breaking the atmosphere if you or your team feel like you're wading through treacle or if difficult events have taken their toll on everyone:

✓ **Suggest an offsite activity**. Sometimes just getting everyone together outside the workplace environment will lighten the mood and encourage some relaxation. There are scores of third-party businesses that offer a whole host of team-building activities or "away days". If this isn't your thing, or if budget is an issue, why not simply have the whole team go out for lunch together? A local pub or restaurant is all you need to change the atmosphere and make the break from your desks.

✓ **Hold a retrospective**. This is a tool taken from scrum project management (and is also, not entirely coincidentally, something we love to facilitate with our teams!). A retrospective meeting allows teams to put down tools and have an open and frank discussion about how they are (or aren't) working together. It results in action items that the team commit to as a group, for things that are in their own power and ability to improve or change. It can be an effective way to diffuse a bigger argument or prevent one from even taking place. Encourage a light-hearted retrospective format so that team members think about the positive stuff they do together as well as the negative (if you want to learn more, "Agile Retrospectives - Making Good Teams Great" by Esther Derby is a good place to start).

✓ **Introduce an off-the-grid day at work.** Allow your team the opportunity to spend a day working on something that isn't related to their current project. It could be something they've always wanted to do but never had the time for, such as learning a particular software package or going on a training course. This is an opportunity to develop a new skill and spend time learning or getting up to speed on something that wouldn't normally be a priority for them. Even just one day doing something completely different can help change the mood, the motivation and the enthusiasm of your reports. They're able to be creative, spend time doing something relating to personal interests and return to their normal job more satisfied and feeling valued by you and the business.

✓ **Just change things up!** Put some music on (without inciting an argument about the playlist), take an early lunch...if it's a small team, you or the business could even pay for it. Give your reports permission to leave early or cancel meetings for the afternoon. Whatever it takes, sometimes a change is as good as a rest...you'll allow people to calm down, recharge and hopefully come back with a more positive attitude.

These are just our ideas based on things we've tried with our teams, but it's by no means an exhaustive list. A bigger one is only limited by your imagination and creative thinking. Don't be afraid to do something different or change the "status quo". It might take numerous attempts of rethinking to achieve your preferred outcome, so be prepared to play the long game. Tenacity is something a good People Manager develops. Persistence is what helps them improve. Determination gives them the ability to succeed.

Summary

- When it comes to dealing with difficult conversations, we find that having a clear framework to follow or a step-by-step guide to keep the conversation focused and on track is always useful.
- It's always better to have a difficult conversation than to avoid an issue; conflicts left to fester will get worse and be harder to resolve the longer they go on.
- Different management styles suit different situations - you can learn flexible skills to help you defuse and resolve conflicts in the workplace.
- It's okay to not always be everyone's friend, and, of course, you won't always be liked - find a style that helps you be a great People Manager and gain respect from your reports and peers.
- Things rarely work out the first time! Don't get disheartened, always be willing to change. After all, you can't make an omelette without breaking a few eggs!

References

1. *80% of Your Culture Is Your Founder* - First Round - https://firstround.com/review/80-of-Your-Culture-is-Your-Founder/
2. *Coaching, Managing or Leading* - PMI - https://www.pmi.org/learning/library/leading-coaching-managing-hat-wear-6029

GROWING YOUR TEAM

Chapter 6

*T*here will come a time when your team needs to grow - and that's a good thing! Adding new recruits to a team can be a rewarding process, and if done correctly, can help the existing team flourish and learn new things.

In this chapter, we'll look at the importance of the hiring process and how you should pay particular attention to it. We'll also lift the lid on the first few months of a new recruit and how you can ensure that they hit the ground running with a solid onboarding process. This chapter is all about growing your team.

Why hiring matters

Great teams are capable of producing something that an individual working alone could never do. If you've been lucky enough to be on a team that gels and works well together, you'll remember the warm, fuzzy feeling you had when everything clicked. It's hard to put your finger on what makes that moment happen, but the heartbeat of any team is controlled by the individuals who make it up, each with their own strengths and weaknesses.

If you browse the web and most bookstores today, you'll find myriad publications about building teams and recruiting staff, but they all seem to lack a few crucial bits of information. Where do you *find* talented staff?

Once you've made a hire, how do you *retain* that person? How do you help them *develop* or grow in their role? All of these questions are important to answer if you want to build a strong team and ultimately contribute to a successful company.

If you've never been involved in hiring individuals before, the concept might seem like a simple one: surely all that's involved is selecting a candidate with the appropriate skills and adding that person to the team? But it's not quite as simple as that! Competition for good talent is fierce, and hiring the wrong person can be detrimental in a team environment, not to mention time-consuming to fix.

Let's be honest, no one teaches you how to recruit or hire staff in school or college, but we're here to help!

Create a plan

When it comes to the new role you're hiring for, have you truly thought about the person you want? This is an important question to answer before you meet potential candidates. If your organisation has a recruitment website, it might be worth your time to personally write the job description so that you have a clear idea of the perfect fit. Once you've done this, run it past your team and get their take as well. It always helps to have a few eyes look over a job description to ensure that you're covering all the bases (especially from those people who will be working alongside this new person).

Develop a good relationship with your recruiter

If you're lucky enough to work in an organisation that uses recruiters or talent acquisition teams (either internal or external), we can't stress enough how important it is to develop a good relationship with them. Yes, recruiters around the world don't always have the best reputation and can be known for their cut-throat techniques, but investing time in building a good working relationship with them can make your life a *lot* easier (plus that reputation is not always deserved).

Whether you're recruiting for one or several roles, organise regular catch-ups to stay in the loop at every stage of the process. During hiring rounds, it's often helpful to arrange regular, short meetings with all the stakeholders involved.

Don't wait to be pestered by the recruiting team - even during busy periods, it pays to quickly check in with them. Working together effectively involves communication and a common understanding of what you're trying to achieve. Recruiters are often happy to help the hiring manager, so checking in regularly can only help improve the entire process for both of you.

Respond quickly

As busy as things may be, hiring should be a top priority, and getting your feedback over to the recruiter right after you interview a candidate can speed up the whole process significantly. Regardless of whether the candidate was successful in the interview, a quick response lets the recruiter understand whether to continue the process.

Even though it may be for short bursts of time, think of the recruiter as part of your team. Things will work much more effectively if you're in sync.

Get the team involved

It's worth remembering that the new hire will be an integral part of your team, so what better way to ensure that they have a flying head start than to include the team themselves in the hiring process? Not only will your team feel like they're involved and responsible from the get-go, but letting them have a say in a potential hire also ensures that you keep things transparent. Together, you can discuss the strengths and weaknesses, talk about why each candidate has been chosen for the interview and collectively choose (or reach consensus about) the best possible candidate fit.

Finding the right person

From the very first moment that a potential candidate comes into contact with your company, they begin to build an idea of what your organisation is all about. What does this company believe in? What are its values and mission? This is why it's so important to clearly communicate those messages. Remember that not only are you interviewing a potential new hire, but they're interviewing you, too - this is a two-way process! Competition for talent is fierce, so you have to sell yourself just as much as they do.

If you have your company values and mission clearly defined from the start, you can filter out candidates who aren't a good fit and save yourself some time in the long run. Any public-facing material should be aligned and clearly communicate company culture.

As you can probably imagine, face-to-face interviews with candidates are an opportunity to learn more about them and *their* values. What motivates this person? What do they care about? Asking questions such as, "What are you most proud of?", "What type of culture do you thrive in?", "How would you describe our culture based on what you've seen? Is this something that works for you?" and "What are you looking for?" are just a few examples of questions that allow you to find out more about the candidate's core values.

If you'd like to dig a little deeper and learn more about getting the most out of face-to-face interviews, my book entitled **Building Great Startup Teams** *is a great place to start!*

It's also worth going a little further and finding out if the person is actually interested in the industry you're in. For example, if your organisation is involved in sports, it might be worth determining if your candidate is a fan as well. Establishing why someone wants to work in the same industry can help you understand if the applicant shares the values of your organisation or is just looking to make a quick buck. Questions such as, "What do you like about this company?" or "Why do you want to work here?" can help you understand whether the candidate is sincerely interested in the job and will be motivated to perform if hired.

A huge part of our adult lives is spent at work, so when deciding if you should hire someone, it's worth determining if this person can contribute to the organisation's success, both in terms of product delivery and overall office culture. Once you begin to align your hiring practises with your company's core culture, you'll find that it becomes easier to screen potential candidates. And when there's harmony between the individual and your culture, there's a greater likelihood that the candidate will feel connected and want to stay.

If you assess cultural fit throughout the recruiting process, you'll hire professionals who thrive in their new roles, drive the success of your organisation and ultimately save you time and money.

Your new hire

Now that you've hired the best talent, it's time to set them loose and allow them to realise their potential within your organisation. With a great onboarding process in place, your new hire will experience a reduced learning curve thanks to a rock-solid onboarding process, the correct equipment from day one, a list of FAQs, a buddy system and a quick lunch or coffee breaks. If you keep those practises in place for every new hire, you'll notice that your new employees become effective, contributing members of the team that much quicker.

Build a rock-solid onboarding process

Our journey so far has hopefully given you some insights into how People Managers can build and sustain happy, healthy teams that are able to achieve their best. Whilst you might have a group of happy reports at the moment, a new person will inevitably join the team and change the dynamic. Their first impressions of your organisation are vital to their long-term success, but you can set them up for success even at the earliest stages in their recruitment. This is where a robust and effective onboarding process comes in.

Modern companies around the world are realising that the transition phase for a new employee is vital. Regardless of whether you're a small startup or a large organisation, new hires need to be nurtured in their first few weeks if they're going to hit the ground running and adopt open, growth-oriented mindsets.

According to Wikipedia[1]:

> *"Onboarding, also known as organizational socialization, refers to the mechanism through which new employees acquire the necessary knowledge, skills, and behaviours in order to become effective organizational members and insiders".*

In essence, onboarding lets you introduce the new employee to your organisation and give them all of the knowledge and tools that they need to be successful. Many companies will have a different approach to it, and the length of the process may also differ, depending on company size. However you approach the process, it gives you the perfect opportunity to continue from a great hiring experience into an even better first month.

Regardless of whether you choose to spread the onboarding process over one day or many, it should cover a few basic things, such as strategy, formal structures and who to go to under different circumstances. But a good onboarding process is also capable of showing the new hire so much more.

As well as being informative, it should be enjoyable[2]:

> *"69% of employees are more likely to stay with a company for three years if they experience great onboarding".*

Before your next employee starts, ask yourself what that person needs to be successful. In addition, ask your current employees what they wish they had known sooner and adapt your onboarding process accordingly.

To get a better understanding of the whole business, have the new hire spend time with a different leader from each department each day. It doesn't have to be a lengthy meeting; rather, it should be a chance for each leader to proudly talk about what their department and team work on. By getting the chance to connect socially, your new hire will better understand office culture and politics. If you have a lot of departments, or if your workforce is split across continents, stick to a couple of leaders instead.

Earlier, we talked about the importance of hiring for cultural fit. The onboarding process is the perfect time to continue this and align the new hire with workplace culture. What is your company all about? What's important to its success? As your organisation grows and scales, strategy will only get you so far: the culture will create a meaningful purpose and bond teams together to fight through tough times.

Not only does onboarding help employees, but companies reap the rewards, too. If the process is done correctly, it boosts your new employee's morale, which in turn increases their overall productivity.

It's worth remembering:

> *You never get a second chance to make a first impression.*

It may seem obvious, but increased morale also lowers the chance of the new employee leaving shortly after joining.

Procure the correct equipment before day one

You should aim to ensure that every new hire is able to get up to speed as quickly as possible, which directly translates into ensuring that new hires have all the tools at their disposal to perform their job from day one.

If your organisation uses computers, ensure that the new hire has simple things such as a fully functional computer with basic account settings and tested equipment, a corporate email account and relevant ID cards. The same is true if your organisation uses machinery and tools: making sure that the employee has everything they need can go a long way toward getting them up to speed right away. Not to mention the fact that it'll help the person feel valued knowing that you've been preparing for their arrival. We can't tell you how many times we've seen organisations fail at this. If you're an employee who arrives to no basic equipment (especially if you accepted the position two weeks ago), it can be pretty discouraging.

Build a list of FAQs

Regardless of whether they're toughened veterans or raw newbies, employees always have common questions. A useful way to help them easily access this information is to create a list of frequently asked questions (FAQs). Add them to the company intranet or even give employees a copy when they first join to serve as a useful reminder.

In a small organisation, you might not have enough information to fill an entire handbook, but a collection of some of your most common questions and answers will be a great help to employees. When reviewing a new recruit's first few weeks or months, it can be enlightening for you to hear about their experiences joining your team. It gives you insight into what really matters to new starters. They may have a flashy new monitor on their desk or a new company-branded water bottle, but if they couldn't find the email address for the IT helpdesk, or if nobody showed them where to go for lunch, their first few days may not have been as good as you had planned. Why not encourage them to update the FAQ themselves, therefore keeping it current and relevant for the next hire?

This kind of documentation is really useful for People Managers because it helps you learn what's important to your employees. Think of it as a guest book at a holiday property: by reading the comments or suggestions, you can refine, improve or change your processes and keep them constantly up to date and agile.

Assign a buddy

Finding the best lunch spots, determining how to order office supplies and knowing who to ask about a specific issue are all important questions, especially if you're a new hire in your first week. While some of the answers might not belong in a list of official FAQs, they're the kind of questions that someone with local experience will be best placed to answer. Accordingly, it's a good idea to assign each new employee a "buddy" that the newcomer can comfortably ask questions no matter how trivial.

Every new team member, regardless of previous experience, should be assigned a buddy. Some companies will purposefully assign buddies from another team or department; this serves as a great way for the new hire to meet new people outside of the team and widen their sphere of influence. However, assigning someone from the same team also works really well if you're trying to reduce the learning curve.

It's up to you to decide how long the buddy should be assigned to new hires. Many organisations aim for a full month, but we would recommend a week. It's important that the new employee doesn't become too reliant on the buddy and is able to grow on their own. Another good idea is to check in with the buddy every now and then to get feedback about how the new hire is progressing.

Grab lunch or a coffee

On their first day or week at a new organisation, a new hire might not get the chance to meet everyone they'll be working closely with. If budget permits, get the team together and take everyone out for lunch with the new person. It's easier for them to relax and enjoy the company of their new team in a casual environment.

If you prefer to keep things a bit more low key, give the buddy an allowance to take the new hire out for lunch or coffee. It's another chance to break the ice and let them learn more about the finer subtleties of your organisation away from desks and computers.

Create a new employee questionnaire

Another great way to introduce new employees to the company is to use a questionnaire. For example, you could create a standard list of questions that asks the employee a little bit more about themselves, almost like a short magazine interview.

Some questions might include:

- What are you currently reading?
- What did you do at your last company?
- What would be your ideal Sunday?
- What are you currently listening to?
- What is your favourite TV show?

While these types of questions might seem a bit silly, they can be a fun excuse for employees to chat with each other and introduce themselves. Once they've completed the questionnaire, distribute it to the rest of the organisation. I've even seen some companies take this a step further and publish answers to their public website!

Core values

From hiring to onboarding, a team's culture and core values are what help retain talent as well as keep them motivated year after year.

So, what exactly are "core values"? Core values are the guiding principles or code of conduct upon which a company was founded and operates under on a daily basis. Rather than these core values being vague ideas or a notion of what good teams look like, they should be a real, daily part of the organisation and woven through everything you do.

To give you a more solid idea of what they are, let's take a look at a great real-world example of core values. Atlassian are an enterprise software company that develops products for software developers, project managers and content management.

Their values are communicated and given to each and every employee from day one. Figure 6.1 lists them: "Play, as a team", "Be the change you seek" and "Build with heart and balance", to name a few. We'd like to think these core values are part of the daily decisions that Atlassian makes, and that every employee is encouraged to keep them at the forefront of their daily workplace activities.

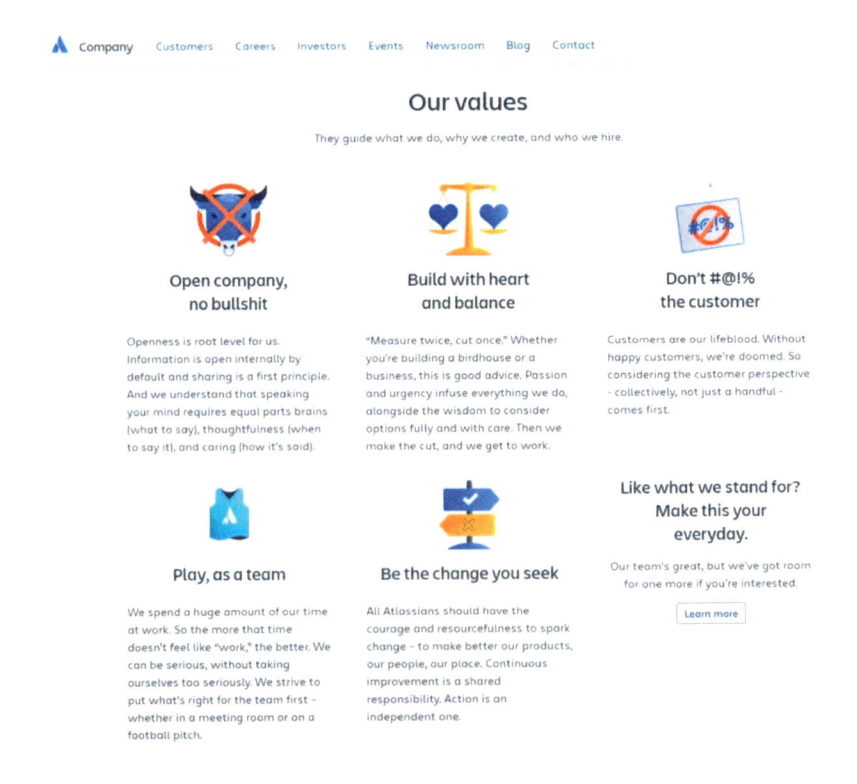

Figure 6.1 The Atlassian website proudly displays its core values on its website's careers pages and in all job descriptions.

While these core values are specific to Atlassian as an organisation, they play a key role in everything the company does. If you browse the career section of the website, you'll easily spot these same values, as well as any open job listings.

Every organisation has different core values that ultimately drive its mission and success, and it's important to understand the pivotal role they play in recruiting. While yours might not be the same as Atlassian, ensuring that they're embedded in both hiring and onboarding can make a big difference in the calibre of people you end up with. Being open and transparent about your core values also means that every candidate who walks through your doors understands exactly what you're *really* about. Translation? If their values match yours, it saves you a mismatch right from the start. Good collaboration, teamwork, respect and pride are that much easier to achieve.

What does this mean for me?

At this point in the book, you might be wondering what core values have to do with you, personally. After all, in a large organisation, you can seem pretty far down the food chain and unable to influence these things. Conversely, you might be in a smaller organisation such as a startup and wonder if you can actually use these core values in your day-to-day work. They might seem a bit daunting, but if you look a little closer, core values actually make your job a lot easier!

For example, utilising the core values of your organisation to frame the conversations you have with your people is an effective communication tool. In earlier chapters, we talked about giving feedback - it's not easy to do it if you're flying blind, but if, say, a core value of your organisation is around "teamwork", and one of your reports hasn't been working as a team player recently, connecting that behaviour to what your company values can be a good starting point.

In Chapter 3, we covered a concept called the People Manager loop. Let's take a look at Figure 6.2 to remind ourselves of this concept.

THE PEOPLE MANAGER LOOP

DAILY → **WEEKLY** → **YEARLY**

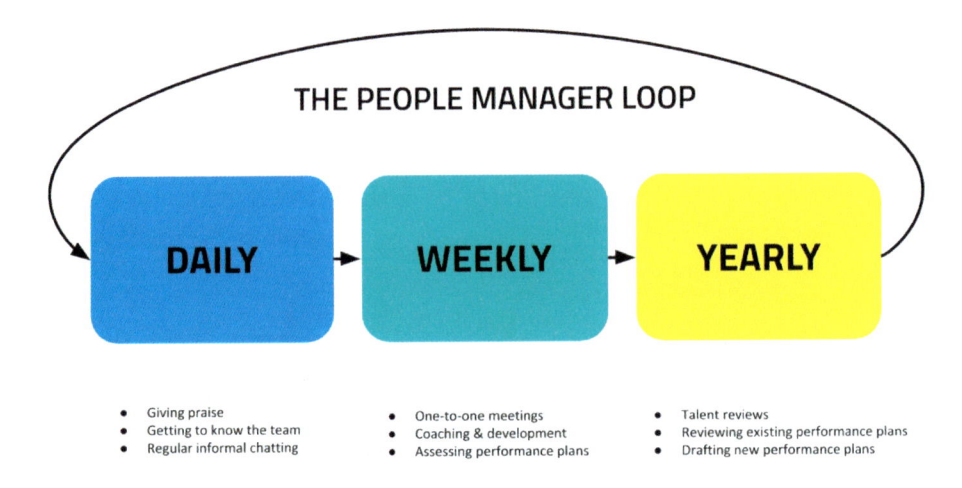

- Giving praise
- Getting to know the team
- Regular informal chatting

- One-to-one meetings
- Coaching & development
- Assessing performance plans

- Talent reviews
- Reviewing existing performance plans
- Drafting new performance plans

Figure 6.2 The People Manager loop.

There are a lot of events and meetings that take place in your daily, weekly and monthly calendar. If you think about how you can use the core values of your organisation to frame these meetings, you're that much more likely to deliver a consistent message to everyone. No matter the size of your organisation, if every People Manager delivers the same message, that message will unite everyone under the same cultural umbrella.

The core values of your organisation are there to provide guidance in making decisions and allow you to be consistent with everyone. If every problem is handled differently (or even in an opposite way from a past, similar problem), teams grow uncertain about what to do next time.

Summary

- When it comes to hiring new candidates, the best thing you can do is to be actively involved in the hiring process and dedicate the time it needs to succeed.
- Develop a good working relationship with your recruiter. Working together effectively can ensure that you quickly and efficiently hire the best person for the role.
- During the hiring process, try and align with the core culture of your company; you'll find that it becomes easier to screen potential candidates for a cultural fit.
- One of the best ways for new hires to learn about your organisation is through the onboarding process.
- If the onboarding process is done correctly, it will boost the new hire's morale, which in turn increases their overall productivity.
- Core values are the guiding principles or code of conduct upon which a company was founded and operates under.
- The core values of your organisation are there to provide People Managers with guidance in making decisions and bring consistency to everyone.

References

1. *Onboarding* - Wikipedia - https://en.wikipedia.org/wiki/Onboarding
2. *Don't Underestimate the Importance of Good Onboarding* - SHRM - https://www.shrm.org/resourcesandtools/hr-topics/talent-acquisition/pages/dont-underestimate-the-importance-of-effective-onboarding.aspx

Chapter 7

IMPROVING YOURSELF

So far, we've talked a lot about how to create, foster and nurture relationships on a team. But someone's missing - and that "someone" is pretty instrumental to the success of all the relationship-building mentioned up to this point. Yes, we mean *you*! Have you heard the phrase "eat your own dog food"? It's a colloquial term, used in business when companies try or test their own products, the idea being that you won't know if you're producing the right thing unless you try it yourself. This term may have been born in the software development industry, but why should it be any different for your own soft skills and practises?

In this chapter, we help you shine a spotlight on your own career and self-improvement because even the smallest change could have a big impact on performance (both yours and your team's). We also explore different approaches to personal growth, such as receiving feedback and working with a coach or mentor. Finally, we examine other areas for growth, such as books, conferences and even online courses. This chapter is all about you (finally).

Feedback

Self-improvement doesn't happen by accident or even by default. The successes and failures of the coaching methods you use, as well as the feedback you proactively canvass (and act upon), mean that you're continuously learning and adapting in your role. Yes, feedback is just as vital for you as it is for your reports!

In Chapter 4, we talked in depth about the power of feedback and the ways to deliver it to maximise its positive effect. But how often have you asked for feedback about yourself? Perhaps you've received the unsolicited type in the past, maybe via word of mouth or by overhearing comments between other people. This kind of feedback can be hard to hear and even harder to act upon - it's out of context and potentially a reaction to a recent issue in the team.

Conversely, it might be the case that you've never received any feedback. How are you going to know if you're doing "the right thing", the "wrong thing" or the "right thing in the wrong way"? This is when you need to seek feedback. Invite comments, constructive criticism and observations on all aspects of your management style. You might feel like you're doing great in your role, that everything's running smoothly, which is fantastic - all the hard work you've been doing is paying off! Do you need to change or improve anyway? Why not try to make your best even better? In the same way that you're continuously encouraging your reports to refine and advance their performance, turn the focus on yourself to find out what areas you could boost or improve. This results in a great deal of "hands-on experience" for you that's worth its weight in gold as you learn from, adopt, iterate on and actually improve yourself and your role. And it's okay that it's like this. If we as People Managers don't remain open to (or actively push for) personal development opportunities and continuous improvement, how can we expect it of others?

The importance of continuous improvement

For top-performing companies, "continuous improvement" isn't just professional business jargon: it's an important, ongoing action, based on feedback from across the entire organisation. Top performers at such companies are not only good at accepting feedback, they deliberately ask for it because they know it's only helpful when it highlights weaknesses as well as strengths. Obtaining constructive feedback is a powerful addition to your toolkit, so what's the best way to get it? Contrary to what you might assume, feedback isn't hard to give - it's all around us in business and social environments. Every time you participate in a meeting, a client discussion, planning session or group presentation, you're engaging in conversational feedback.

Different businesses have their own processes and tools to help employees of all levels set goals and have meaningful conversations with their People Managers. Goal-setting meetings and frequent coaching help us stay focused and accountable so that we can perform at our highest level. One of the great things about having a feedback-gathering program is that you can ask pretty much anyone you know in the company to participate. If your company doesn't have such a process already set up, we encourage you to look into putting one in place.

This kind of specific feedback often takes place each quarter throughout the year (every three or so months), and it's a time when employees can reach out and ask for what they need to help them improve. This is a successful method because it can be anonymous – it's gathered by each employee's manager to discuss with them without necessarily disclosing the person giving the feedback. The feedback provider can be honest and comment on real issues, achievements and behaviours without pressure. Having a regular cadence also means that providers aren't saving it up for a year, they have the opportunity to share smaller, more regular observations that can be discussed and acted upon more quickly.

Of course, feedback will be positive in the areas where you've made a good impression or produced great results. Everyone needs (and benefits from) "feel-good feedback" - it acknowledges a job well done and helps embed the working practises you've been using.

However, if the only feedback you receive are glowing testimonials, does that really help you identify areas to focus on in your mission to improve yourself? Probably not. To pinpoint what you need to work on, you need to ask specific questions of your feedback providers. Consider putting together a short survey or tailor some questions to send out with your request that will enable the recipient to comment on specific areas of your work, projects or personal style.

For example:

"I'd like you to give me feedback on my role this year" - this is a very generic request for feedback that will result in open-ended commentary about whatever the provider feels they should say. Or (worse), they won't know how to answer, so they won't say anything!

"I'm interested in how you feel I have performed as your manager this year, thinking specifically about one-to-ones and my communication style" - this request immediately tells the provider what you want to know about. They can spend time giving a more focused reply, which will ultimately be far more useful for you to hear and subsequently act upon.

If you want a wider "zoomed out" view of your performance as a People Manager, asking simple questions can give the provider a bit more creativity with their responses:

"What did I do well over the past 3 months?" "What should I stop doing?" or even "What should I start doing?" are great questions to show that you're genuinely interested in hearing how you can improve your performance. You'll earn respect not only by asking these questions but by listening/accepting the responses and ultimately acting upon them to make a difference.

Reacting to negative feedback

When you've made the decision to request feedback on yourself as part of your self-improvement, receiving negative comments or criticism can be an unwelcome shock or surprise. You'll find yourself in defence mode, where you'll want to refute the feedback, deny it or challenge the truth of it. You may be unaware that any improvements were even needed! But take a breath - this process is all about learning and growing. It's time to decide if you're ready to own your actions and open yourself to finding resolutions that can help you along the journey to becoming the best People Manager you can be.

It's human nature to feel embarrassed in the face of negative feedback or that your pride (or ego) have been dented somewhat. The most important thing is what you're going to do with this feedback to improve yourself.

Step one: Resist the urge to deny it immediately. You asked for feedback, and you got it. Think about how you can take it on board and understand what information it gives you to work with.

Step two: Try not to get distracted by questioning the origin of the feedback. Its purpose is to help you focus on what you can change to become a better manager. Instead, reframe the feedback you've been given - work out why this setback or stumbling block might have occurred at this particular moment. Caution: this is not the time to unpick who gave the feedback (going on a witch hunt is counterintuitive).

Step three: Think only of positive change! How can you change your actions or behaviour to achieve an actual improvement? Think about moving forward rather than looking back (or standing still).

Step four: Find a way to summarise this process for your own learning benefits. Tempting though it is to continue to justify that your way of doing things is right or that others are at fault, how does this attitude help your growth mindset? If you feel like you *are* always right, you'll only seek out the feedback that supports that belief. But think of the useful and genuine information you'll miss out on, all of which will help your ongoing career growth and personal development. As a People Manager who seeks to always improve and learn, strive to accept negative feedback when it happens (hopefully not too often) as helpful rather than hurtful.

Coaching and mentoring

Professional sports teams and individual athletes work closely with coaches to improve their game. Coaches are able to assess from a bird's-eye view and help address any weaknesses.

Which is why it only makes sense that if you wanted to improve as a manager, you might want to consider coaching. After all, if you wanted to be a world-class golfer, you'd go for golf lessons...right? Even top pros such as Tiger Woods work with a coach to ensure that they're at the top of their game and can make small tweaks to improve their game. Executives, CEOs and managers all over the world also work closely with coaches and mentors to ensure that they're able to improve daily. According to research from the University of Georgia[1], employees who receive mentoring achieve higher positions, pay and career satisfaction. Those all sound like good reasons to us!

The difference between coaching and mentoring

Coaching or mentoring? What's the difference, and does it really matter? We touched on these terms briefly in Chapter 5 when we talked about coaching versus leading. We like to think of mentoring as a partnership in which one person shares knowledge, skills, information and perspective to help the personal and professional growth of someone else. Mentors are typically outside the mentee's immediate team, not in their reporting line. A good example of someone who might make a mentor could be someone who has worked in your industry or someone with experience in your role who can guide you. They'll be able to give you feedback based on their own experiences.

Coaching, on the other hand, is slightly different in that it's typically done by someone external to your organisation. Business coaches might be people who've been trained for this and charge for their services. They don't necessarily have a background in your role; rather, their goal is to help you get the best from yourself, without telling you how to do so! Historically, organisations used to hire business coaches to come in and fix broken executives. Nowadays, most companies hire business coaches as a way to invest in their top executives and junior/mid-level managers. Having a business coach is no longer seen as a bad thing - it's an exciting opportunity!

Is this really for me?

After reading this section, you might be wondering if getting involved in mentoring is really the right thing for you. After all, you might have only recently been placed in the role of People Manager and are still finding your feet. You might even have bought this book with the intention of learning more about what being a People Manager entails. Don't be put off!

True, mentoring isn't for everyone, and it might be too early to tell if it's right for you, but it's worth keeping in mind for the future. If you reach a point in your career where you feel that you want to grow and push yourself, a mentor might be how you do it. If world champions at the top of their game still use coaches and mentors, shouldn't you consider it, too?

Figure 7.1 If you reach a point in your career where you feel that you want to grow and push yourself, a business coach or mentor might be a good next step.

Regardless of whether you decide that you're ready to work with a mentor or coach, it's important that you approach the concept of outside help with an open mind. You'll be pushed outside of your comfort zone because a good mentor or coach *should* challenge you in ways that you might not have experienced before. You might even end up with feedback about yourself that you won't necessarily like. With all of this in mind, taking feedback on board can be the best way to grow and improve yourself, and we hope we've convinced you to embrace it.

Becoming a mentee

If you're familiar with the *Star Wars* films, you're probably familiar with the concept of Jedis and Padawans (if you aren't familiar, basically, a Padawan is an apprentice who hopes to one day be a Jedi). Under tutelage from a Jedi master, Padawans learn and grow, and it might seem like a silly analogy, but the comparison works quite nicely when you're thinking about mentoring. In this context, you would be the Padawan, and your mentor would be the Jedi master!

Having a mentor who is experienced in your industry or role - someone who can also provide you with honest feedback - will go a long way in helping you continuously improve. Right now, you probably feel like a Padawan with a lot to learn, so it makes sense to find a Jedi who can guide your path.

Mentors come in all shapes and sizes, and they can be found either inside or outside your organisation. If you don't have someone specific in mind within your organisation, consider looking further afield, such as business associations in your area, non-profit organisations, your college or university, your family or even chambers of commerce. One thing to keep in mind is that a mentor should be someone who is genuinely interested in growing you. You should never, *ever* have to pay for a mentor.

Once you find someone who's interested in being your mentor, what next? We recommend that you start by answering the following questions and discussing them with your mentor as you figure out your overall plan:

- What is your current situation?
- What is your vision, or what do you hope to achieve?
- What is your career goal?
- What knowledge do you want to gain?
- What skills do you want to build?

To get the most out of your mentoring experience, it's critical to establish needs, set priorities, identify timeframes and define goals. You'll revisit this stage as the relationship develops, your trust grows and you continue to establish development goals. This approach will also help you focus the conversation on exactly what you want to achieve. You want advice, but you also want to frame that advice.

It's best to set a schedule for regular check-ins (aim for once each at 3, 6 and 12 months) so that you can monitor your progress. You need to understand what you've learned, how you've benefited from the experiences you've had and what skills you've built. Asking questions will help you assess where you are and where you've been as you continue to evolve your mentoring relationship.

We could probably write a whole book on the many different approaches that can be used when mentoring. We don't want to prescribe the best approach, but rather open your mind to the possibilities and advantages that it could bring.

If you do consider mentoring, try to keep an open mind, and your potential to learn and grow will truly be unlimited.

Working with a coach

Business coaches are often from an external company that is paid for their services. Unlike a mentor, you might find that the business coach runs this role as a full-time job and helps many organisations, not just yours. As an objective outsider, a coach is free to question you on major issues, obtain valid data and address specific issues.

Another great thing about working with them is that different coaches specialise in different subjects. Where one might be an expert in public speaking techniques, another might be more accomplished in strategy and management and yet another could be the perfect person to help you manage your time more efficiently. Coaching can also provide you with a safe environment to reflect and refocus on confidential issues. They can act as a sounding board, a function that tends to be less regular and harder to find the more senior you become. Whatever area you're looking to improve in, you can be sure that there's a coach with the skills to work with you.

Because business coaches are paid professionals, each one will have a set format that they'll use when they work with you. The process is similar to mentoring (establishing needs, setting priorities, identifying timeframes and defining goals), but it will take on a different variation depending on your needs.

The process is typically over once the development goals are achieved or when you and the coach decide that the engagement can end.

After a few years of being a People Manager, I felt that I needed a little guidance to push myself further. I felt like things were plateauing in my career, and I wanted to get out of my comfort zone.

I have to admit, I was quite wary at first about working with a coach and was nervous to say the least! After finding someone with the right background, we got started with regular check-ins. Fortunately, the coach was easygoing, and we clicked straight away.

It was uncomfortable at times, and I was definitely outside of my comfort zone, but I'm happy to say that it pushed me to learn new things that I would never have done otherwise. I would definitely recommend coaching to anyone looking to grow as a People Manager!

It's worth keeping in mind that a coach should be guiding you to unlock potential within yourself - if you find that you aren't getting the best out of the relationship, perhaps it's not working, and that's okay, no need to keep going.

You might be lucky enough to work for an organisation that will pay for your coaching, but if that isn't the case, consider paying out of your own pocket. All in all, coaching is designed to help you succeed as a People Manager, so there will be certain skills you'll need to develop in order to succeed and flourish. If you find that you want to challenge yourself and take your career to the next level, keep coaching in the back of your mind!

Learning and growing

In previous chapters, our focus has been on helping you grow the careers and skills of the people who work for you, but it's also important to remember that you need to do the same for yourself. You've spent countless hours hiring, assessing and nurturing great talent - now it's time to do the same for yourself! There are plenty of tools available to you so that you can continually refine, expand and improve your own skills and abilities. Here are just a few.

Books

During our careers, we've noticed that different people prefer different mediums to learn something new. For example, you might like reading books to expand your knowledge, whereas someone else might prefer to watch online videos.

Whilst reading a lot of material (whether in print, on a kindle, or via audio) might not necessarily be on your radar, it's worth mentioning that for a relatively small price, a book can be a low-cost way of learning valuable knowledge from some talented authors. In fact, it might be worth finding like-minded people in your organisation or friendship group who are interested in learning more about leadership that you can share books with. It's a great way to access a wider library and be inspired by others at the same time.

In this particular book's appendix, you'll find a list of some of our favourites. We recommend picking a few that catch your eye!

Conferences

Conferences let you engage with other people and learn from them at the same time. In fact, attending a conference and seeing how other leading organisations are building their businesses can be a great way to keep yourself excited about your own role. Large conferences with respected speakers offer the perfect opportunity for you and your team to learn from some of the best minds out there.

Public speaking doesn't fill everyone with delight, but it's worth mentioning that another great way to challenge yourself is to speak at a conference.

As you learn more about people management, the things you take for granted could be shared. Who knows, your story might inspire others out there, too!

Online learning

Another great medium for learning is the web, especially if you're tight on time and money. There are a plethora of websites, blogs and online training courses that can help you grow in your role regardless of your industry. We're both big fans of online learning as it can be done at a convenient time with little disturbance to your day-to-day work. You can log in for an hour or two at a time and top up your skills as needed. Some of our favourite online learning providers include Coursera.org and OReilly.com, to name two.

Another great way to keep up to date with industry trends is to subscribe to different blogs and newsfeeds. Many business bloggers write about the daily challenges they face as People Managers, so this informal platform can be a great way to learn tips and tricks from other industry leaders.

Maintaining perspective

To grow the people around you, you need to grow yourself. To support your efforts in this endeavour, it's important to pay attention to your work/life balance, which boils down to keeping a sense of perspective in what you're trying to achieve or work toward.

It's a hackneyed phrase, but what exactly do we mean by work/life balance? In a nutshell, it means dividing your time, energy, focus and attention between work interests and family/leisure time. Wikipedia sums this up nicely[1]:

> *"Work–life balance is the lack of opposition between work and other life roles. It is the state of equilibrium in which demands of personal life, professional life, and family life are equal".*

To give the best of yourself, you need to make sure that you're both mentally and physically in good shape, that you aren't burned out. We aren't saying that you shouldn't put in hard work when a project requires it, but rather to do so wisely. Tough times will require superhuman effort, with late hours and early mornings, but this shouldn't become the norm. It's important to find a healthy balance between challenging yourself, having your team's best interest at heart and burning yourself out by getting the balance wrong.

Figure 7.3 I'm too busy for a burnout!

Your reports look to you, their manager, for guidance. If they see you crunching away the hours, emailing late at night or behaving in an overworked, stressful way, they might assume that this is what you expect from them as well. You're setting an example that just isn't sustainable, and you won't perform at your best or get the best from your team on top of that. Too much effort can actually become counterproductive. When you and your team sacrifice too much time and energy, you've most likely decreased your productivity and output. This breeds resentment and stress, and ultimately may mean that your team choose to work elsewhere.

Obviously, we don't work with you, so we can't prescribe the best methods for achieving a good balance - it's different for everyone. What we *will* prescribe is that you try to remember to protect your own well-being and that of those around you. Take breaks and relax (yes, it's allowed!), encourage humour in the workplace, eat and drink with your team, get enough sleep and take time to think about and do things (other than work) that make you feel alive. By making these small changes, you'll return to work more engaged and productive each morning, which will in turn inspire those around you and promote a happy and healthy culture amongst your teammates.

Summary

- Constructive feedback for People Managers is a powerful tool that can help you improve and grow.
- Having a mentor who is experienced in your industry or role can go a long way in helping you continuously improve.
- Business coaches are paid professionals who have a set format they use when working with you.
- Coaching can provide you with a safe environment to reflect and refocus on confidential issues.
- It's important for you to step back and realise that to grow the people around you, you need to do the same for yourself.
- Many different tools can be used for your continued growth and education, including books, online learning and even conferences.
- To avoid burnout, aim to create a balanced culture and environment where employees aren't expected to work ridiculous hours. Remember to set the example yourself!

References

1. *Work–Life Balance* - Wikipedia - https://en.wikipedia.org/wiki/Work%E2%80%93life_balance

MAINTAINING A HIGH PERFORMING TEAM

Chapter 8

Up to this point, we've focused on finding your feet as a People Manager and taking those early steps with your direct reports. We've also looked at the more practical side of people management, which involves performance management, building teams and dealing with tricky moments. Now it's time to take a closer look into the longer-term side of people management - i.e., how you maintain a high-performing team for the future.

In this chapter, we explore the benefit of reviews and explore tools such as the 9-box grid and 360 Feedback to ensure that you fairly, openly and objectively appraise your people. We'll also describe how to maintain a high-performing team by looking at how to reward great talent.

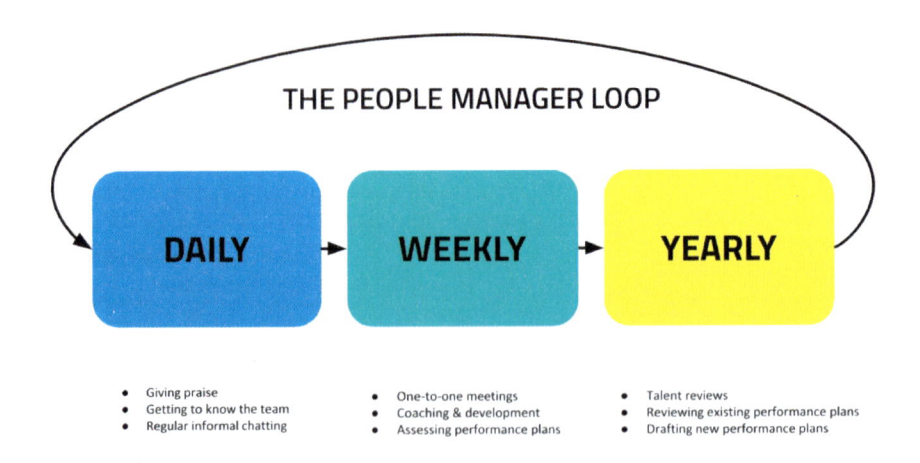

The People Manager loop

Before we go any further, let's cast our minds back to the People Manager loop that we went over in Chapter 3. In your role, there will be things that you do daily, weekly and even yearly, but it's important to understand how all the pieces fit together and when you should be doing what.

Figure 8.1 reminds us of what the People Manager loop looks like.

THE PEOPLE MANAGER LOOP

DAILY → **WEEKLY** → **YEARLY**

- Giving praise
- Getting to know the team
- Regular informal chatting

- One-to-one meetings
- Coaching & development
- Assessing performance plans

- Talent reviews
- Reviewing existing performance plans
- Drafting new performance plans

Figure 8.1 The People Manager loop.

In the loop above, the cadence of events is something that we find works well for us, but you can adjust to whatever works best for you and your business. We'll focus in this chapter on some annual tasks that you might perform. These tend to occur less often, but they're still vitally important to the health of your team.

Talent reviews

Whether you work with a large team or a small one, it's important to keep that team's long-term health in mind, but how do you do that? Talent reviews are the answer. Depending on your organisation, you may already have some type of talent review in place. Some organisations like to do their reviews every 6 months, others every 12, but regardless of cadence, talent reviews help strengthen your team and reveal weak spots that may need addressing.

But what does "talent review" actually mean? Put simply, it's a chance to take stock of the people you have working for you and to review (or measure) them against your expectations. Are they succeeding in their role? Have they improved over time? Are there areas for development or even a change of course? Conducting these reviews regularly enables you to maintain a good level of understanding about performance. We like to perform these reviews once a year, with smaller check-ins at the end of each business quarter, but you can adjust to your own needs. Let's look at some of our favourite techniques and tools for talent reviews.

The 9-box grid

Perhaps you've heard of a tool called the 9-box grid - it's a mapping tool used by many organisations to assess how their team members perform in a comparative way (you map current performance against potential).

The 9-box grid can be a great way to review each member of your team and get a sense of the overall "health" of their skills and performance. For example, mapping your team may reveal that you have a lot of individuals who have high potential but aren't performing well. This might be something that you need to look into.

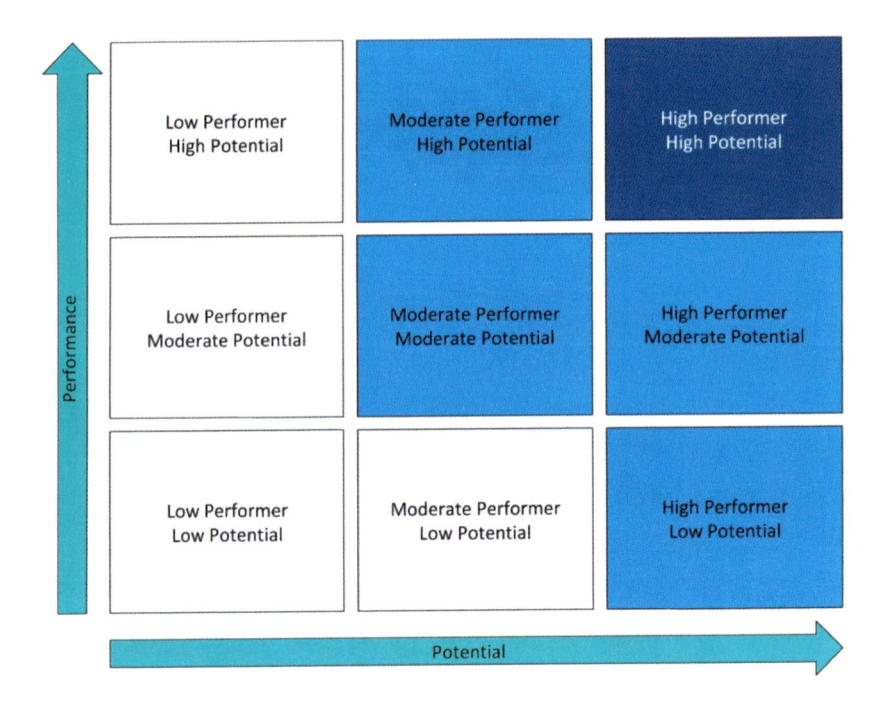

Figure 8.2 The 9-box grid.

Let's review the 9-box grid in Figure 8.2 and break it down so we can see how it works. As the name suggests, it's a scaled matrix of 9 boxes that allows you to map your team members according to how they currently perform and their potential for future performance. The further up the grid someone is placed, the more impressive their performance has been since your last review; in the same way, the further to the right that someone is placed along the grid, the more potential you're saying they have.

Let's imagine you have a team member called Lisa. She's a great team player and consistently produces good results. She's also an up-and-coming star with great potential. Given her performance this past year, you might place her in the top right corner of the 9-box grid under *High Performer, High Potential*. Your business model can then decide what the next step should be: promotion, bonus, salary increase? Placing a report in this box highlights that they have the ability to achieve more or have outgrown the role that they're currently performing.

Next, let's imagine you have another team member called Greg. He has shown moments of great potential, yet has performed poorly since the last review. With this in mind, you might place Greg in the *High Potential, Low Performer* box, which flags Greg as someone who needs close attention. It's worth catching up with Greg and finding out what might be the cause. If you can see that his potential is high, yet you aren't seeing real results, then a conversation needs to be had. Is he doing work that motivates him? Are there difficulties that prevent him from achieving more? All of this is a springboard for further discussion.

We love that a tool such as the 9-box grid can give you the ability to get a snapshot of the health of your team at a quick glance. For People Managers, there's nothing more rewarding than identifying someone who's struggling, working closely with them to turn it around (provided that they're willing, of course!) and moving them into the top right corner.

Performing these reviews regularly is such a valuable process. If you let each year pass by without taking stock of your team, their health and performance, cracks can start to develop that could have been easily avoided. Not only do you have no way to detect poor performance, but you also can't recognise and reward good achievements. What you do with this information is up to you and your company, but it's a great exercise to carry out for staff appraisal, development and reward.

We're both big fans of the 9-box grid, but it has to be said that not everybody is! First and foremost, the output is extremely confidential. This information is subjective and personal, and if shared with anyone other than leadership/HR peers, it would be a serious breach of confidentiality and data protection.

In addition, measuring potential and achievement can often be quite difficult and subjective, depending on manager and employee expectations and personal goals. Wherever possible, it's always worth collectively running through a 9-box grid exercise with other People Managers. This gives you the opportunity to justify the placings, discuss the data or examples that you based them on, verify the feedback together and validate your grid.

360 Feedback

Within our roles as People Managers, one of the most useful tools we use is 360 Feedback, a method of performance appraisal that gathers feedback from several contributors, including peers, managers and even customers.

The idea behind this tool is that, on a regular cadence (yearly, biannually), you gather feedback from multiple sources for each member of your team. This feedback should be confidential (and unless the provider specifically says so, you shouldn't share who gave it). Why? The feedback given will be more honest and candid if it's anonymous. It will also help raise issues that would otherwise be uncomfortable to state publicly and ultimately of no help to the recipient.

The great thing about this feedback is that instead of a one-dimensional view, you're able to form a much more rounded opinion based on multiple points of feedback from the people who work closest to the person, hence the name! Ultimately, it's not *your* opinion, it's the opinion of the employee's peers. If you've ever had to deliver tough feedback to a report, it can be a lot easier when you know the feedback is coming from the team (with examples) and isn't only your (quite possibly subjective) opinion.

In its simplest form, 360 Feedback questions should give the person giving the feedback the opportunity to comment on positive behaviours and work achieved over the past few months, as well as suggesting things that could be improved/changed.

The sample questionnaire gives an idea of what this might look like:

Feedback for Jane Doe	
Question	**Reason**
Going forward, what would you like to see the employee **keep doing**? *Be specific and include examples about what this employee can continue to do to be effective in his/her role.*	The aim of this question is to find out what the person does really well in their role and what other people see as their strong points.
Going forward, what would you like to see the employee **do differently**? *Be specific and include examples about what this employee can do to be more effective in his/her role.*	This is a chance for others to suggest things that they think the person could improve or start doing - a springboard for goals or personal development.
Do you have any additional feedback you would like to provide about the employee?	This could be an acknowledgement for a particular behaviour, or it could be constructive criticism about something that might have gone unchecked.

Once this feedback has been collected from a number of sources, the information can be compiled into a solid, constructive and useful summary. Keep an eye out for recurring feedback from more than one source. For example, if multiple people are saying the same thing about someone (albeit phrased in a different way), it's worth digging deeper and bringing it up with the person during a feedback session. In this scenario, having an idea of the impact the behaviour has had/is having will help you communicate the feedback more clearly. Of course, it doesn't always have to be negative feedback, it can be multiple instances of positive feedback that you might want to encourage and definitely make a noise about!

Another key area to look out for is negative or overly critical feedback given by only one individual. Sometimes this could be due to a personality clash or even a historical grudge that hasn't been resolved. Other times, it might be a genuinely legitimate piece of feedback that needs to be heard. Reading through the responses to requests for feedback and sifting between the lines is a skill you'll need to master!

It's also important to ensure that feedback is timely and frequent. You might find that conducting 360 Feedback too regularly might be time-consuming. It puts pressure on the same contributors and may not yield particularly useful comments. From our experience, once a year is an ideal cadence. It can be tied into the annual appraisal process and allow people who have worked with your team members over the course of a whole year to contribute.

Ultimately, there are no hard and fast rules about how often feedback should be requested and given. Some employees want it throughout their time spent on projects - their passion for learning and growing means that they want to know how they're doing and what they can improve. This is great! Take the lead from your reports and see what works for them.

It's also worth mentioning that some great software products can make this process a lot easier. HR software can be automated so that feedback request/return occurs on a given time schedule and remains anonymous when received. Workday and Culture Amp are just some of the products out there that can make this task easier for People Managers.

Delivering 360 Feedback to an employee

Now that you have all of this great feedback, it's important to ensure that you deliver it in the most useful, productive way. As we've pointed out, regardless of whether it's positive or negative, the results of 360 Feedback should always be anonymous. If it's negative and a name is associated to it, this feedback can cause hostility in the office and possibly grudges. It's also worth omitting specifics related to projects that could make the source seem obvious; in addition, you'll want to make sure that feedback sources are diverse, not just friends of the employee.

In our experience, 360 Feedback works well when delivered verbally. Each point can be discussed, perhaps referring back to a specific point in time related to it. The employee should have their say, especially if you're bringing development opportunities up or criticisms of something they've done (refer to the "Difficult conversations" section in Chapter 5 for advice here). Importantly, they may not - and do not have to - agree with all the feedback, and that's okay, you can discuss it further at a later point.

Feedback about behaviours that others notice but the person denies is an interesting conversation to have. We can't stress this enough, but examples are the key here. You want to provide examples as well as the negative impact that this behaviour has. You can't expect someone to understand feedback that has been given about them without an actual example to illustrate it. All feedback should be written down for the employee to refer to at their leisure. It could be as part of an appraisal form or simply an email that you've made sure is an anonymous summary of what you've communicated.

The power of praise

Whether you're the CEO or leading a small team, praising an employee goes further than you think. In fact, giving someone praise will actually boost morale and improve employee satisfaction. A recent study by the O.C. Tanner Institute found that 7 out of 10 employees who report they've received some form of appreciation from their supervisors say they're happy with their jobs[1].

As an employee yourself, you know it doesn't take a genius to work out that receiving praise feels good. But as a manager, it's so easy to forget to praise people for a job well done. Too often, we think that monetary rewards will make someone feel valued at work. Some of the best managers we've ever seen were quick to praise and reward good work. The truth is that giving employees recognition will help you engage with them, retain them and even accelerate their performance. The best thing about it is that it's free!

In Chapter 4, we talked about some of the best times and ways to give praise to someone. If you notice that someone has done a good job or has been struggling with something and finally achieves it, take note of it and let them know. Don't limit yourself to the people you manage: anyone you work with is worthy of praise for a job well done. Before you know it, you'll have added to a positive culture in your organisation.

As we've progressed through this chapter, we've focused on 360 Feedback and the 9-box grid, but remember that good feedback should come from these exercises, too! It feels good to get praise from your manager, but it feels even better from your peers. When delivering feedback, take care to separate positive and negative comments and to not mix or blur the message in a confusing "feedback sandwich".

Motivating others

Maintaining a high-performing team takes a lot of focus and dedication. Using the tools described above, you'll be in a good place to really understand not only the performance of your reports but also what motivates them to be the best version of themselves. Sustaining this level of motivation as well as growing it can be done in a variety of ways (most of which will depend on the policies and processes in place in your organisation):

- **Money.** Without getting into financial details, it's worth understanding whether your reports are being paid a fair salary or a contract rate that's comparable with other people doing the same role elsewhere. Does your compensation scheme reflect personal achievement in the form of discretionary bonuses, stock awards or other rewards? If your reports feel that they aren't rewarded fairly for the work and efforts they put in (and you agree that their contribution is high), you might want to look at how your business can correct this. However, not everyone is motivated by money[2]:

> *"Money encourages self-serving short-term behaviours better than it motivates lasting institutional achievement".*

Of course, we aren't suggesting that money doesn't motivate. It's a critical part of the hiring and retention of good employees. Beyond that, being motivated solely by financial reward tends to be a self-serving motivation. Team members who feel respected, admired, trusted to do a good job, fulfilled in their role and recognised by peers and leaders tend to display far greater motivation and enthusiasm for their job.

- **Personal development/career growth**. Regardless of whether your talent reviews or feedback gathering yield great results or opportunity for improvement, your reports will hopefully be motivated by capturing these acknowledgements and actions in a development plan. Linking achievements to goals or objectives might seem like an overly simplistic way to chart personal growth, but over time, this record provides a motivational way to show progress.
- **Motivating workload**. When your reports achieve great things in

their daily tasks, don't make drastic changes to their role. Of course, every business has to respond to changing priorities, to marketplace and industry challenges that can alter the course of the work that has to be done. However, if your team members are enjoying the work they do, produce great results and add value to the business, be mindful of messing with success. As with many other People Manager tasks, this is a conversation. Talk to your reports about the work they're doing regularly and check that it remains a source of inspiration, enthusiasm and productivity. Although it might not always be possible, doing your best to ensure that they get to work on things that bring out the best in them will give them confidence in you as a manager and ultimately maintain their high performance, which is a great outcome for them, for you and for the business.

Summary

- Talent reviews can help strengthen your team and help you find weak spots that may need addressing.
- The 9-box grid is a tool used by many organisations around the world to assess how their teams are performing. The grid places an individual based on their past performance and helps show an overall view of the health of your team and the actions you should take.
- Regardless of your role in an organisation, feedback is a critical part of your growth and development.
- 360 Feedback is a method of performance appraisal that gathers feedback from a number of sources, including peers, direct reports or even customers.
- Even the humblest of people appreciates being praised for hard work!
- Once the performance of your team is at a high level, maintain and improve it further.

References

1. *The Easiest Thing You Can Do to Be a Great Boss* - HBR - https://hbr.org/2015/11/the-easiest-thing-you-can-do-to-be-a-great-boss

Chapter 9

LOOKING TO THE FUTURE

We can't quite believe it, but we've arrived at the final chapter of this book! Hopefully, we've inspired you with ideas, tools and processes to put to good use in your new role. We've covered some of the things that you might face in your early journey, but before we sign off, we'd like to share some things that we wish we were told when we became People Managers!

We'll start with a brief recap of the book and highlight some of the most important takeaways. Then we'll talk a little about why staying positive is one of the most important mindsets you can adopt as a People Manager. Finally, we'll finish with some words of wisdom that we hope you'll be able to put into practise going forward.

Key takeaways

It's difficult to know what to include and what to leave out - all our experiences have been valuable to us as People Managers, and we want you to benefit from what we've been able to share with you. Before we go any further, let's pause and recap some of the key topics that we've explored. If you take nothing away from this book other than these things, then we'll have achieved our goal as authors (and fellow People Managers!).

1 to 1s/1:1s/one-to-ones

We cannot stress enough the importance of catching up with your team through regular one-to-one sessions. In Chapter 3, we delved into the importance of these sessions and how to get the best out of them. One-to-one conversations are the best opportunity you have to build rapport and trust with your direct report, to learn first-hand what motivates, inspires, frustrates or even angers them. So, although the one-to-one meeting helps you as a manager, it's also incredibly important for the development and job satisfaction of your team members. In fact, done well, one-to-ones can inspire team motivation, confidence, loyalty and productivity.

These meetings are the single most important thing that you can do as a People Manager. We know it sounds as if we might be overstating the point here, but in our experience, it's the truth. If you feel like you need to brush up on getting the best out of your one-to-one sessions, revisit Chapter 3. One-to-one sessions are by far our favourite topic. If you feel nervous, unsure or even doubtful about the potential value of having one-to-ones, just try it. We guarantee that even if it's something very small, you'll see a benefit straight away.

Receiving praise

Regardless of whether someone is a seasoned veteran or a newcomer, everyone likes being praised. In Chapter 8, we explored the power of praise and why giving it to someone is proven to boost morale and improve employee satisfaction.

But you don't need to go around showering everyone with random compliments and praise (overuse can have the reverse effect of making your comments disingenuous or meaningless), rather, you should save them for a job genuinely done well. If you aren't used to doing this as a manager, it can feel a little awkward at first, but we promise that your words will encourage your team. As the saying goes, *it's better to give than to receive*, and believe it or not, you might end up enjoying it more than you think. Never underestimate the power of praise!

Don't lose your cool

We'll be the first to raise our hands and admit that we aren't the best at keeping our cool when faced with challenging or difficult situations. If you're passionate about your job, when times get tough and pressure or stress becomes too much, it can be difficult to stay calm. However, in hindsight, losing our cool has never served us well!

In Chapter 5, we covered some of the techniques that we like to use when times get tough and we're dealing with conflict in the workplace. Whether this conflict is between yourself and a report, between two members on your team or is just a tough situation, it's important that you don't shy away from the problem at hand. Your team are constantly looking to you and assessing how you react to different situations.

If you get angry and express that anger in the wrong way, it can only serve to make you look worse - even if you're right (or at least feel like you're right). It can be hard, but if you feel a red mist descending, simply press pause, excuse yourself from the situation and literally leave the room. Take a walk, grab a coffee or find a colleague or other manager who can act as a sounding board or voice of reason. If possible, sleep on it before you approach the issue again. Sometimes this isn't possible, and issues need dealing with immediately, but forging ahead when you're angry or frustrated won't allow you to deal with it in the best way. Revisiting the issue with a clear(er) head will let you reframe it and keep your calm. No matter how you personally feel about things, approaching them calmly and dispassionately is always the best and most professional method.

Be yourself

If you're stepping into the role of People Manager for the first time, without any prior experience or training, it can be intimidating. But once you've found your feet and feel more confident, it's important to always be an authentic leader. What do we mean by this? Well, an authentic leader is simply one who is always themselves. In the workplace, it can be easy to try and emulate other managers' styles, but the reality is that no one can be authentic by trying to imitate someone else (it will also be mighty difficult to keep up appearances!). You can learn from others' experiences, but there is no way that you can be successful when you're simply mimicking them. When we think back on our careers, the people we most trusted were those who were genuine and authentic. We liked them, we trusted them and ultimately, they helped us grow.

In the very first chapter of this book, we asked you to think about your values and what really motivates you. Once you discover *what* drives you and *why* you get up in the morning, you'll be a step closer to becoming an authentic leader.

However, there's another side to being an authentic leader: showing vulnerability. Regardless of whether you're the CEO of a billion-dollar organisation or a People Manager in a small startup, it's always worth remembering that you're human and prone to weaknesses and mistakes.

By being real and admitting your shortcomings as a leader, you'll subconsciously build trust with your team and show your human side. After all, no one wants to work for a perfect robot!

Great people managers care about hiring

There are so many things that we do daily that are vital to the success of our organisations. While all of these things are important, none of them are actually possible without *people*.

It reminds us of one of our favourite quotes from the book, *The Hard Thing about Hard Things*, by Ben Horowitz[1]:

> *"We take care of the people, the products and the profits...in that order".*

If you analyse the quote, it might seem a bit strange. When times are busy, and it feels like everything around you is manic, it can be tough to stop and take the time to focus on hiring. As the pressure piles on, it can feel like a luxury to give the hiring process even a few spare minutes of thought. But having the wrong people in your company directly impacts your ability to create and deliver results. Without a motivated and successful team in place, you'll simply end up spending even more time spinning on the spot and trying to accommodate new work requirements and incoming challenges. The right people in the right place can make all the difference to your own ability to deliver on your commitments to your business.

Dean Says

I have to admit that I'm a little biased about the hiring process. My book **Building Great Startup Teams** *focuses on hiring and building teams in smaller organisations.*

During my time as a manager, I've noticed that not everyone gives hiring the same attention that it deserves. It's often seen as an unnecessary distraction, but this shouldn't be the case! Hiring is one of the most important things that you can do. I truly believe that building a great team starts with finding the right people!

Jo Says

Believe me, Dean takes the hiring process very seriously! But all joking aside, since working together, we've invested a lot of time into refining, developing and iterating on the recruitment processes we use. Early in my career as a People Manager, hiring seemed a "necessary evil", something no one really wanted to stop their day job to do.

Time spent trawling through CVs, phone screening and interviewing seemed to fall way down the list of interesting or important tasks. However, as we talked about in Chapter 6 of this book, working with talent acquisition, HR, other managers and colleagues to invest time in how you recruit and the kind of people you want to join your team really does pay dividends when you have fabulously talented new recruits join

Whether you're experienced at hiring people or brand new to it, you know in your heart of hearts that hiring people takes time. And if you're looking to hire the *right* people for your business, it can take even more time. There's no formula or recipe for success when it comes to hiring. But trust us, hiring the right people requires time and attention to detail that will ultimately pay off in the long run.

Staying positive

In his book, *First Man In: Leading from the Front*, Ant Middleton explains why the power of staying positive has been so important during his career[2]:

> *"No matter how much trouble I've managed to get myself in, the only way I've ever got myself out of it is by keeping a positive mindset".*

Having served three tours in Afghanistan (as well as being an ex-SBS sniper and Special Forces Operative for the British Military), Ant has experienced the highs and lows of working on a team under tough conditions. We aren't suggesting that you apply a military mindset to your daily work (that might be a little extreme), but take a leaf out of his book and apply a positive outlook to your workplace.

If you think about it, negativity is an obsessive distraction. When you're in a negative mindset, it's easy to focus on the bad and find every excuse available as to why things aren't working out. The reality is that you can only focus on one thing at a time (including negative things), so once you go positive, you can now apply the same mental capacity in that direction instead.

Whether you face tough issues at home, in your personal life or even in the workplace, it's crucial to remember that people are looking up to you. Your actions and how you portray yourself play a big part in this. If you're negative, your teammates will feed off it and react the same way. It's really hard to build happy teams when the person managing them isn't happy!

Never stop learning!

The primary focus of this book is on your early months and years as a People Manager. Let's fast-forward a few years and imagine that you're now a successful People Manager who's doing a good job in your role. But once you've been established for some time, it can be easy to slip into a false sense of security and assume that you don't need to keep your skills sharp. After all, you're doing a great job, *right!?* Well, this may very well be true, but it's still important to keep pushing yourself to improve in your role.

Remember that the role you're doing **right now** is active learning: every day, you're absorbing different experiences, trying out different tactics and adopting new skills that you might not have had yesterday. Don't beat yourself up if you've had a tough day, week or even month! We learn from our experiences, good or bad. The parts of your role that challenge you are the ones that will help you grow and push you to the next level. Always have a growth mindset and regularly ask yourself, "How could I have handled that differently?", "Who can give me feedback that I can use in my development?", "What can be done to improve xyz?" But also be sure to pat yourself on the back with personal acknowledgements: "It was difficult, but I did a great job", "I made a real difference to that person/project/situation", "I've come a long way since I took on this role, and I'm proud of what I've achieved!"

In Chapter 7, we explored different approaches to personal growth such as receiving feedback and working with a coach or mentor. We also looked at other avenues for growth such as books, conferences and even a myriad of online courses.

Our advice to you is to continually seek out ways to keep improving, whether that be yourself, your skills or even your confidence in the role that you're performing. Sometimes self-improvement is as simple as reading a book about something that inspires you. You've made a good start by choosing to read this one!

In the appendix, we've added a list of our favourite books that we highly recommend you read. Some of them we've referenced here, but others are great business books that are among our must-reads. Not all of them are strictly people management related; rather, they focus on teams and people in business.

And finally...thank YOU!

We hope we've been able to support you - not only with our own experiences and learnings (because not everything has always gone smoothly for us) but also with our suggestions, ideas and inspirations for how you can maximise your own skills and grow into your new role. Now it's over to you. Ideally, this book has provided a useful framework for you to build upon and adapt your own leadership style. Have confidence, be bold and believe in your abilities - we wish you luck in the next chapter of your career!

Summary

- One-to-ones are the best opportunity you have to build rapport with your direct reports, to learn first-hand what motivates, inspires, frustrates or even angers them.
- People are the most important part of your business and can be the difference between a good product and a great one.
- There's no formula or recipe for success when it comes to hiring. Building great teams requires time and attention to detail, which will ultimately pay off in the long run.
- Keeping a positive mindset in the face of tough challenges will help you through them as well as let your team shine at the same time
- Once you've been established in your role for some time, it can be easy to slip into a false sense of security and assume that you don't need to keep your skills sharp. However, it's important to keep pushing yourself, to continue to improve in your role.

References

1. *The Hard Thing about Hard Things* by Ben Horowitz - HarperCollins - 2014
2. *First Man In: Leading from the Front* by Ant Middleton - HarperCollins - 2018

Further READING

When we set about writing this book, we created it based on the experiences we've had, people we've met and things that we've learnt along the way. It's also fair to say that a lot of books have influenced us and helped formulate the thoughts we've laid out on these pages.

The books below are some of our favourites that we highly recommend reading:

The Carrot Principle: How the Best Managers Use Recognition to Engage Their People, Retain Talent, and Accelerate Performance by Adrian Gostick & Chester Elton - 2009

Beautiful Teams: Inspiring and Cautionary Tales from Veteran Team Leaders by Andrew Stellman & Jennifer Greene - 2009

The Hard Thing about Hard Things: Building a Business When There Are No Easy Answers by Ben Horowitz - 2014

Dare to Lead by Brené Brown - Penguin Books - 2018

High Output Management by Andy Grove - Vintage Books - 1995

The First 90 Days by Michael Watkins - Harvard Business Review Press - 2013

The Making of a Manager: What to Do When Everyone Looks to You by Julie Zhuo - Portfolio - 2019

HBR's 10 Must Reads on Leadership by Various Authors - 2011

The Practice of Management by Peter F. Drucker - 1954

Never stop learning!